THE
SCIENCE AND PRACTICE
OF HUMILITY

"With the clarity of an eagle soaring in the still peace of a clear blue sky, Jason Gregory offers us an important work in the development of a vision of unity and peace. *The Science and Practice of Humility* is a revelation, speaking to that inner knowing that has never been separate from who we are and have always been. Gregory's style is both intellectually stimulating and personally evocative. This book is a treasure to hold in two hands: to ponder, to enjoy, and to allow its alchemy to call upon that which is our best, and our salvation."

ROBERT SACHS, AUTHOR OF
BECOMING BUDDHA AND *THE ECOLOGY OF ONENESS*

"A profound and important book. From his exploration of Hermetic principles and the true meaning of alchemy, to his deconstruction of false ideas of manifesting wishes, Jason Gregory makes a unique contribution to an evolving philosophy for the 21st century. This eminently readable and thought-provoking book renders a service to us all."

GRAHAM HANCOCK,
AUTHOR OF *SUPERNATURAL:
MEETINGS WITH THE ANCIENT TEACHERS OF MANKIND*

"*The Science and Practice of Humility* acts as a bridge between East and West by presenting Oriental wisdom to the modern world. This is a profound book with a simple and clear explanation of some of the classic concepts of Oriental philosophy."

SATISH KUMAR, AUTHOR OF
THE BUDDHA AND THE TERRORIST

THE
SCIENCE AND PRACTICE
OF HUMILITY
The Path to Ultimate Freedom

JASON GREGORY

Inner Traditions
Rochester, Vermont • Toronto, Canada

Inner Traditions
One Park Street
Rochester, Vermont 05767
www.InnerTraditions.com

Text stock is SFI certified

Library of Congress Cataloging-in-Publication Data

Gregory, Jason, 1980– author.
  The science and practice of humility : the path to ultimate freedom / Jason Gregory ; foreword by Daniel Reid.
    pages cm
  Includes bibliographical references and index.
  ISBN 978-1-62055-363-3 (paperback) — ISBN 978-1-62055-364-0 (e-book)
  1. Humility—Religious aspects. I. Title.
  BJ1533.H93G72 2014
  205'.699—dc23

                                                              2014006410

Printed and bound in the United States by Lake Book Manufacturing, Inc. The text stock is SFI certified. The Sustainable Forestry Initiative® program promotes sustainable forest management.

10 9 8 7 6 5 4 3 2 1

Text design and layout by Debbie Glogover
This book was typeset in Garamond Premier Pro with Hypatia Sans Pro, Helvetica Neue LT Std, and Gil Sans MT Pro as display fonts

To send correspondence to the author of this book, mail a first-class letter to the author c/o Inner Traditions • Bear & Company, One Park Street, Rochester, VT 05767, and we will forward the communication, or contact the author directly at **jasongregory.org**.

Dedicated to the humble hearts of the sages
and those of us who trail
the footsteps of those masters
into the chamber of that sacred abode

Contents

It's All in Your Mind

Daniel Reid

*D*arwin was wrong about the basic dynamics of evolution. Evolution is not driven by the adaptive development of bigger fangs, sharper claws, and faster feet. It's driven by the evolution of consciousness. All of the physical forms of life on Earth and the myriad functions of nature manifest and change continuously by virtue of an invisible template of consciousness that is constantly evolving at the source of their creation.

If big fangs and sharp claws determined the "survival of the fittest," then the human species would long ago have been devoured by tigers and torn to shreds by wolves, disappearing without a trace from the face of the Earth. Instead, humans have become the king of the jungle, lording it over all other species.

Conscious life on Earth evolves in a cyclic spiral of ever-accelerating velocity, and we have now reached the point where consciousness is evolving as much in a single year as it once did in a million. The Stone Age evolved at a slow crawl over a period of

3.5 million years, while the subsequent Bronze Age zipped by in only 2,500 years, followed by the Iron Age in just 500 years and the Industrial Age in less than a century. In the current Age of Information, human consciousness has already evolved more in a mere 20 years than it did in all previous ages combined, and the pace continues to accelerate.

The fast rate of development in computer technology today is one obvious example of how rapidly evolving consciousness manifests in new material forms and functions. It took a million years for a better design of stone arrowheads to be developed, but today it takes only a few months to develop superior software for your computer and phone. A major contributing factor in the incredibly rapid evolution of consciousness that we are experiencing today is an unprecedented rise in the vibrational frequency of the entire planet, which began during the last decade of the twentieth century and continues to accelerate today. This ambient global frequency is known as the Schumann Resonance, and all life on Earth is subject to its influence. Over the past twenty years, it has almost doubled, thereby expanding the spectrum of conscious awareness, stimulating the development of new ideas, and awakening dormant functions in our DNA. As a result, not only are we consciously transforming the physical world in which we live faster than ever before, we are also gaining new psychic abilities that we never even imagined we had.

Quantum physics has proven that all matter ultimately boils down to bundles of energy condensed into patterns that our physical senses perceive as solid matter, producing an illusory view of material form that we call "the world." In reality, all physical forms and functions in the world, including our own bodies, exist by virtue of rhythmically vibrating energy. The driving force that orchestrates this vast symphony of organized energy, which we know as "the world," is consciousness. By the application of conscious intent, spirit mobilizes the infinite potential energy of the universe to create all the manifest forms and functions of life. Molecular matter is composed entirely of subtle organized energy fields that appear to our minds as physical forms ranging from the size of an atom to that of a star. Each form has its own unique energy patterns, its own individual energetic rhythm, and its own signature vibrational frequency.

Whether we can hear it or not, all vibration produces sound, so this ongoing process of creation manifests first as invisible sound and then as the visible light of form and function. As the Bible states, "First there was the word." The ancient Hindu and Buddhist masters agree with this view, telling us that the world manifests from moment to moment as energy organized into fields of form, by virtue of sacred syllables such as *om, ah,* and *hum.* Dzogchen teachings state that the infinite potential energy of primordial awareness manifests first by virtue of sound, which then refracts clear light into the five colored rays that constitute the five elements of creation. Essentially, the entire manifest universe is an eternal song of life that produces a dazzling light show of infinite complexity.

Truth itself is as simple and singular as the sun rising in a cloudless sky, dispelling the dark shadows of night with the clear light of day. What complicates matters is the human mind, which uses the divine gift of conscious awareness to forge a personal ego that serves only the interests of the imaginary individual self. Arrogant and greedy by design, the ego is driven by what the Buddha called "the three poisons"—desire, anger, and ignorance—which blind the human mind to the spark of divine light that lies at the heart of all sentient life, linking us inseparably with all other beings. Like a crazy kaleidoscope, the ego fractures the clear light of primordial truth and reweaves the fragments into complex patterns that reflect its own preconditioned views, suit its own preconceived notions, and serve its own exclusive interests at the expense of all others. The ego always scripts its own story and calls it "reality," constructing an illusory world that conforms solely to its own personal agenda.

Today, as the vibrational pulse of the planet continues to rise and evolution of consciousness accelerates at an ever-faster pace, problems that for centuries have been swept under the carpet are crawling out and demanding solutions. Issues kept hidden within the mind's darkest corners suddenly scream out for answers, and ideas that only recently seemed inconceivable now crystalize clearly on humanity's mental horizons.

People are driven in two opposite directions by this process. Some are drawn like moths to a flame by the luminous glow of enlightened awareness dawning on the horizon; they do what must be done to purify and transform themselves as suitable vehicles for awakened consciousness. This is the path of spiritual self-cultivation. Others cringe at the prospect of shedding their personal agendas and shrink away from the task of subjugating their individual egos to the higher call of universal spirit; they crawl deeper into their dark lairs of familiar old habits, hiding from the dawning light in personal comfort zones where "ignorance is bliss."

The key to catching the rapidly rising wave of evolving consciousness and riding it to the shore of awakened awareness is humility, plain and simple, and that's what this book is all about. Author Jason Gregory, a young Australian with an uncanny eye for truth and a sensitive ear for the song and dance of creation, culls the answers we're seeking today from the vast archives of ancient wisdom teachings that have been handed down to us through the ages but are rarely understood. Guiding his readers skillfully through the rich legacy of esoteric philosophy and spiritual science bestowed upon humanity by the world's greatest minds, he presents us with a clear-cut blueprint that applies the key lessons contained in these ancient teachings to the current task of our own conscious evolution today, here and now.

At his age, Jason hasn't had the time required to spend long decades in solitary seclusion mulling over these weighty matters, as the old graybeard masters did, so somehow he has learned how to tap directly into newly opened neural links that allow him to download insights from the universal hard drive of Source itself.

"Consciousness is not only the foundation of the universe," he states, "but it *is* the whole universe." In that case, we all have the potential capacity to connect our conscious minds directly with the universal Source of all knowledge and wisdom and to search for answers to any and all questions.

Profound implications follow from the insight that the entire universe is not just an arbitrary conglomeration of inert matter, but rather a living, breathing manifestation of conscious awareness that shape-shifts and transforms from moment to moment in accordance with the evolution of the creative consciousness at work behind it all. It means that if we wish to change the world, then what we need to change first and foremost is the consciousness within ourselves, not the external forms of the outside world. One of my own favorite precepts states, "Change yourself and you have done your part to change the world."

The text sparkles with gems of practical wisdom that shed

light on daily life in the world, such as the observation that love and fear function as two psychic poles in life. The chronic fear that most people feel in life today is really just a critical lack of love, a failure to open one's heart to others and to practice the virtue of unconditional love, which melts fear from the heart like sunshine melts frost from the grass. Thus the antidote to fear—and to all the anger, hatred, and aggression it engenders—is love, a humble truth so simple and clear that it's rarely recognized as the true solution to all the machinations of the ever-fearful ego. As John Lennon sang, "All you need is love."

Gregory has a remarkable ability to integrate spiritual concepts from such diverse sources as India and China, Egypt and Greece, and to distill their essence into simple ideas that anyone who reads English can understand without prior spiritual training. He presents us with a nonsectarian summary of all the great treasuries of spiritual wisdom collected through the ages and fuses them with supporting evidence from modern science. The result is a seamless synthesis of Eastern and Western traditions that focuses clearly on the most vital issues facing humanity today.

The insight that evolution is essentially a spiritual rather than a physiological process shifts the primary focus of scientific inquiry from physics and chemistry to consciousness and spirit, and this shift changes the whole picture. It means that consciousness is not a product of brain chemistry, but that brain chemistry is a function of consciousness. It means that you see what you believe, not believe what you see, and that you are more what you think than what you eat. And it confirms the sovereign command of "mind over matter," which means that each of us has the power within ourselves to manifest what we want in life and to reshape the world in which we live.

In his chapter "The Evolution of Perception," Gregory discusses the vital importance of learning to see beyond superficial forms by opening the eye of eternal awareness and thereby focusing consciousness on the primordial light of Source rather than the superficial forms of the temporal world. In Buddhist tradition this sort of vision is known as the Clear Light of Great Perfection—Mahamudra and Dzogchen. To achieve this we must cultivate the intuitive understanding and direct experience of our real primordial condition as formless, luminous beings of infinite potential energy that manifests continuously without interruption. By realizing that in our primordial state we are all one and the same energy, we dispel the illusion of separation of self and other and learn to take responsibility for how we manifest our energy in the world. To do this we must overcome the arrogance of ego and cultivate the virtues of humility and compassion, which allow us to evolve spiritually. True power grows not from the barrel of a gun: it grows from the light that shines from an illumined mind.

The author discusses at length the iconic clash between the way of the sage and the way of the warrior, which manifests in so many ways now throughout the world. In traditional Chinese philosophy, this fundamental dichotomy in human nature is referred to as *wen* (the literary arts) and *wu* (the martial arts), the proverbial contradiction between the pen and the sword. The conflict between the two has determined the course of history in human civilization. Though the sword often gets the upper hand, unleashing the dogs of war, sometimes "the pen is mightier than the sword," and prolonged periods of peace prevail.

These two divergent paths in human nature reflect the polar split between the spiritual and the material aspects of life. This fundamental duality in the evolution of human consciousness represents the clash between love and fear. The struggle between the two has not only been the driving force in the story of humanity, but also causes major conflict within the minds of all human beings. Which of these divergent paths one follows in life depends upon which basic attitude toward the world one decides to cultivate—the arrogance of the warrior or the humility of the sage.

Modern military technology today has grown so viciously efficient at killing people and destroying our natural habitats that humanity can no longer tolerate the indiscriminate death and destruction of rampant high-tech warfare without running the risk of total extinction. The current prevalence of the warrior mentality throughout most of the world today is amplifying this looming threat of annihilation to a critical level.

Humanity has reached a crucial crossroad in its evolution. If we wish to survive and continue to thrive as the master species on Earth, we must cultivate the virtue of humility and apply it as an antidote to the hubris of arrogance. We must learn to illuminate the darkness of fear that provokes violent conflict with the radiant light of love. On our long and winding journey through life, we must always try to tread the peaceful path of the humble sage, yielding to others we meet on the way, and to shun the temptation of trampling tribal rivals on the violent trail of the arrogant warrior.

In the following pages, Jason Gregory adeptly maps the subtle terrain of enlightened awareness explored by the sages of antiquity and elucidates the illumined teachings they left encoded for us in the ancient archives of esoteric philosophy. Along the way he shows us how the simple science of humility serves us as a torch of certainty that lights our way through the darkness of ignorance and how it functions as an infallible compass that keeps us on the straight and narrow path to the goal. His message evokes the spirit of my favorite Tibetan prayer:

Precious Masters, essence of all buddhas
of the three times,
To you we make this prayer:
For the sake of all beings, please cause us
to relinquish ego clinging.
Please cause contentment to be born in us.
Please cause us to perfect the practices of
illusory body and dream.
Grant us your blessings that we may attain
the supreme accomplishment of the
Clear Light of Great Perfection—
Right now, immediately, here in this very
place!

Now is the time, and here is the place. Let's get started!

DANIEL REID has a master's degree in Chinese language and civilization, and he studied Taoist practices in Taiwan for sixteen years and in Thailand for ten before moving to Australia in 1999. He is the author of several books, including *The Tao of Health, Sex & Longevity, The Tao of Detox,* and *The Complete Book of Chinese Health & Healing,* and the translator of *My Journey in Mystic China,* John Blofeld's autobiographical account of his years spent in pre-Communist China.

Acknowledgments

*T*he *Science and Practice of Humility* could not have come to life without the help and support of numerous kind-hearted people who have graced my journey in life. So many that it would be hard to thank all of the amazing people whom I've had the pleasure of meeting, so I can only mention those who have had a direct impact on this book.

First of all most books have no life breathed into them without the expertise and wisdom of a publisher, such as Inner Traditions • Bear and Company. I am especially grateful to Jon Graham for his support of this book and for his recommendation to Ehud Sperling whom I'm thankful to for not only believing in my book, but for also having established a publishing house that is willing to push conventional boundaries. To Meghan MacLean and Nancy Yeilding, my astute editors both with an uncanny eye for literature, thank you for bringing a flow and clear structure to this book, which has made it much more accessible. To all of the other amazing people of Inner Traditions whom I worked with from all departments, it has been a blessing to be involved with all of you and please continue to inspire the world.

I owe a special debt of gratitude to Daniel Reid for taking the time to read this book and for believing in it so much that he wrote a foreword for it. Daniel was instrumental in introducing this book to Inner Traditions for which I am forever grateful.

I must give a big thanks to all of the wonderful people of Tiruvannamalai and Dharamsala in India, Pokhara in Nepal, and Bangkok in Thailand, as these places are where the words of this book came into existence. Thank you for feeding me and giving me shelter, and most of all for being my friends, which was all the inspiration I needed.

A deep bow of gratitude to all of those sages and teachers, from beyond the grave and those living, for blunting my sharpness and for clearing the dirt from my eyes. Though there are too many to mention, I must thank you for untying my wings so I could be set free to fly and share the message of your humble heart with the world. Without your existence this book never would have been written.

The films, lectures, and workshops that make up my work outside of this book have all contributed to it as interconnected steps to the unfoldment of the words in this book. The production side of my films, lectures, and workshops has been blessed by the work, help, and support of Justin Jezewski, John Casey, and Derek Gedney for all of whom I'm grateful to call my friends.

To Janice and Alan Gregory, my beloved mother and father who are no longer with me in this world, thank you for bringing me into this world and teaching me the lessons of life in the multifaceted way you both did. My youth was a joyful time and I have so many fond memories primarily because you were the flame of the candle that illuminated my life. It is a shame that we only got to spend a brief time together, as there is so much I would love to share with you, but everything is for a reason and I now finally know that you never left me. Wherever both of you are, whatever form or plane you reside in, I sincerely hope your journey is an enlightening experience, which I'm sure you share together.

Most of all this book never would have happened without my beloved wife and closest teacher, Gayoung, with whom I am blessed to share this life. My life has changed in innumerable ways since we met, and I have become a more centered and peaceful individual in the grace of your presence. Every day is new and fresh when I bask in the sunshine of your beautiful smile and marinate my soul in the radiant glow of your eyes. Thank you for living an adventurous life with me, meeting the challenges we encounter with a sincere humility that allows us to experience joy more purely. Even though we spend every day together, I never get tired of expressing my love for you.

Introduction

꾟꾟

The Science and Practice of Humility is a book meant to ignite your intuition by connecting you with the consciousness of the enlightened masters of all times. Dwelling beyond conventional thought, a master reveals a science hidden deep within the essence of our being, here termed "the science of humility." If we look into the stories and legends of the past, we find masters and sages all over the world who embodied this science of humility. Ancient China gave birth to the grandmasters Lao-tzu, Chuang-tzu, Lieh-tzu, and Confucius, while in ancient India we find Krishna, Rama, and Gautama the Buddha. Traveling over to the Middle East, we discover the great sages Hermes Trismegistus, Jesus of Nazareth, and Muhammad.

Individuals who practice the ultimate science exist not only in the past but are always with us, as evidenced throughout the twentieth century in sages such as Sri Ramana Maharshi, Thich Nhat Hanh, and the Dalai Lama, to name just a select few. The immense power of the science of humility is easily demonstrated by the fact that the influence of these sages reverberates within the labyrinth of our minds, across space, and through time.

Even though these humble sages throughout history appear so plain and silent, like empty vessels, they somehow transmit knowledge and wisdom that goes beyond the scope of our five senses. The miraculous part of this process is that they do this without the slightest forethought or predetermination, validating something preexistent within the empty vessel of our primordial awareness, pure luminous space that most individuals hurriedly fill with mundane "stuff." Navigating this empty space, in which humility and a receptive approach to life can be allowed to grow unfettered, is a science that one can learn and live by, and that is what this book comprehensively explains.

The fragrance of humility is an art that inspires others to change, brought forth by our enlightened masters from their mystical abode. We don't usually discuss science, art, and humility in the same context. Our modern perception is that science is a form or method of study pertaining to acquiring systematic knowledge through observation and experimentation. But this discounts and leaves out actual experience and the experiencer of the reality. To solve this conundrum, we need to seek out the original and correct definition of science before our modern intellect tampered with it. The origins of the word *science* are the Latin *scientia,* meaning "knowledge," and another Latin word *scire,* meaning "to know." This sheds new light on our modern perspective of science as merely a tool for acquiring facts.

The original definitions of the Latin words describe the experience of the individual and the inner knowledge assimilated from that experience. In fact, in its essence and origins, science has more kinship with the Latin word *omniscient,* which means "having complete or ultimate knowledge and an awareness and understanding of all things." In this context the science of humility is closely related to the school of Hindu philosophy known as Vedanta in Sanskrit. Vedanta is an esoteric path and teaching that corresponds to a scientific method applied to one's own experience. This is why Vedanta is known as "the science of Self-realization." The science of humility revealed in this book differs in the sense that it is the science of the masters who have already attained what Vedanta is seeking: the transcendental state of enlightenment. Though this science may appear vague to our highly intellectual society, it can be understood in light of the Sanskrit concept of *dharma,* "the artistic function of that experiential science possessed by a master," a concept we will explore in detail.

The Science and Practice of Humility reveals the entire process each individual goes through on his way to enlightenment, as it unfolds through three phases or stages of growth: *the great work of eternity, the evolution of perception,* and *the science of humility.* Learning the science and art of an enlightened master is not another way of filling one's mind to the brim with information acquired from external sources, in the vain hope that this will somehow grant enlightenment. On the contrary, it is a process of refining the mind, becoming familiar with the mysterious regions of simplicity within the psyche where the science of humility is spawned. By contrast modern external science is only concerned with the exploration of matter through various definitions of complexity, a process in which we lose sight of and no longer value what in essence is very simple.

The reversal of complexity into simplicity is a process that is resurfacing in the modern era and will continue to unfold in the future. After over-emphasizing the acquisition and decoding of information, we will naturally be drawn to move back toward a simplified way of life and being. But this natural impulse to harmonize with the simple way the universe exists and functions is not universally seen as desirable, as a majority of people believe that success, freedom, and liberty are attained through a complex life. As a result the simple truths that exist in eternity and within all of us are constantly being made complex by our intellect, which attempts to give the intangible a name and form, so we can somehow find meaning to suit the conditioned limitations of our mind.

At the same time, we all know intuitively that there is something deep in the unknowable region of our psyche, something nameless and formless that underlies the fabric of reality. The masters and sages, past and present, have a relationship with that formless unknowable reality. The science of humility is an authentic exploration of that formless simplicity that a master or sage brings to the world, which is something beyond words.

We all have the ability to know the transcendent, but we continue to be drawn into the complexity of our own concrete reality. What we see through our eyes is in essence formless until we project our personal idea on to that formless reality and give it a concrete name and form. The nature of this wrong perception is determined by the indoctrination each individual has undergone since birth. In Hindu and Buddhist wisdom this is known as *maya*, a concept we will discuss at length.

Under such hypnosis we do not realize that what we are using to give definite form to the world is in itself intangible. Though we have the ability as human beings to think, feel, and emote, we do such things in the realm of the mind, which does not even exist within the human body. Although the function of the mind appears to be located within the organ of the brain, in fact it cannot be located there. So the definite form we attempt to give the world is an empty function of the formless mind. The complexity we are drawn to is not something that exists outside of us; it exists only in the way we attempt to give definition to ourselves in relation to the world in which we live. We do this to make ourselves feel that we have a purpose on Earth and to find meaning in our disordered lives.

This is not to say that our individual existence and life itself have no purpose or meaning. On the contrary, purpose and meaning are the very essence of who we really are deep within, not something we need to seek outside ourselves, then arbitrarily interpret and define in form. Our conditioned belief that there is a precisely correct interpretation of life has led humanity into the illusion that the world "out there" exists separately and independently from the individual who observes that world. If both the world and the one observing the world are essentially formless, how could either one be defined in form? Would that leave the nature of the entire universe open to personal interpretation?

Transcending definite form and personal interpretation is the essence of the science of humility, which shows how the essentially formless reality of the universe is experienced differently in manifest form by each individual. *The Science and Practice of Humility* refers to that reality as the *irreducible essence,* something we all intuitively know is beyond words, definite interpretation, and concrete form. Our attempts to attribute solid form and definitive interpretation to that irreducible essence have led many religious and spiritually inclined individuals to give anthropomorphic form to angels, guides, and gods, and, most astonishingly, to intellectually analyze it in terms of structured concepts. This gives rise to religious fanaticism and spiritual pride because such conditioned perceptions are rooted in the illusion of the separation of self and other, form and essence, and the arrogant belief that somehow we can define the irreducible essence as a separate entity with culturally conditioned human qualities.

As we interpret life we are challenged to remain lucid, free of conditioned responses, and wide open to any views and new experiences that might reveal themselves. Otherwise we will be deceived by our own rigid thoughts about how the universe should be, rather than seeing it as it really is. Such rigidity of thought then gives birth to fanatic behavior and the radical separate consciousness that brings violence to our species. In our modern era we see an amazing spiritual awareness evolving, but we still witness the complexities of form and those who seek to define themselves uniquely according to arbitrarily defined parameters. In most cases it doesn't matter if someone is highly intellectual or artistic, an atheist or a spiritualist, because more often than not, most grow proud of their personal level of understanding and their own world view, or preach the superiority of their own chosen particular path and practice. This is nothing more than clinging to an illusionary projection from within their own mind.

Since the dawn of civilization, one of the worst manifestations of such arrogance has been the individual who claims to be an enlightened being, a claim that an authentic master or sage disdains for its gross lack of humility, the most basic virtue of enlightened awareness. Such arrogance easily snares those who are trying to grow consciously, because it traps them within the confines of a definitive interpretation of the manifest world. They end up playing a game of "spiritual one-upmanship" in which they vie with others at intellectualizing the spiritual wisdom of that formless reality rather than being at one with it and simply being its silent expression. There is nothing extraordinary about any of these views, for they are all just arbitrary reflections of the ordinary mundane state of worldly awareness, deluded by an illusionary and superficial complexity.

The science of humility does not complicate the nature of the ordinary individual. On the contrary, as presented in this book, it aims to cleanse the polluted psyche and simplify the ordinary, which thereby becomes the extraordinary. To emphasize this the great Zen Buddhist master Lin Chi said:

> Just be ordinary and nothing special. Relieve your bowels, pass water, put on your clothes, and eat your food. When you're tired, go and lie down. The ignorant may laugh at me, but the wise will understand.[1]

Lin Chi is not saying that one should lead a boring existence and never enjoy the sweet fruits of life. Instead he is saying that, in the basic simplicity of life, extraordinary things will manifest, just as the complex shapes and aroma of a flower bloom from a simple humble bud. All the great sages of antiquity lived within the mystery of this quiet, humble state of simplicity and contentment, and this is what the science of humility explores in its infinite depth. The science of humility also outlines the fundamental structure of consciousness and the eternal principles at the heart of the universe.

Such humble simplicity, matched with profound wisdom of how the universe works, is a state of consciousness foreign to most of us in the modern era. Indeed, we are swiftly losing sight of what is truly important about the basic state of being human. Our simple basic nature has been distorted by our intellect into a complex morass of external forms. The result of this process is the arrogance we show toward the essence of universal reality and our careless disregard for living our lives with the humility required to realize our true human nature. Ordinary sages do not conform to society's psychic state, which ridicules anyone who fails to fall in line with the hypnotic belief that in order to become an extraordinary individual one must lie, cheat, and steal one's merry way to the top of the social heap, and that happiness can only be found in the relentless accumulation of material fame and fortune. In a world such as this, humility is dismissed as a foolish weakness. Society's status quo feels threatened by an intangible force beyond words and far more powerful than material wealth, and so humility is demeaned as useless and mistaken as a form of humiliation.

This arrogant attitude toward humility has become par for the course in modern times, with most people believing that nothing can be achieved or gained thereby. In the Western world this attitude has prevailed for a long time. If the virtue of humility is described as a gateway to enlightenment, the remark is usually greeted with a smirk, as though one were speaking nonsense. The Western intellect has always looked down upon Eastern philosophy because Eastern spiritual thought and metaphysical insights are far too abstract and non-materialistic for the Western mind to comprehend. The common response of the Western intellect to something that it does not comprehend is to ridicule it, which is simply a face-saving device. Though this arrogant attitude toward spiritual virtue was once confined only to the Western world, it has now infected the entire planet with its illusionary spell. Evidence of this can be seen in contemporary China, where Marxist intellectuals ridicule the ancient spiritual path of Taoism, which lies at the very heart of Chinese culture and history. They question how humility can be seen as a virtue and how it can change things for the better. The whole world is blinded by the hypnosis of idle gossip, arbitrary judgment, the pursuit of personal fantasy, worship of external achievement, and the idea that money holds the key to our happiness.

Collectively as a species we pine for equality and an enlightened society, but in our endeavor to bring this to fruition, we individually conspire against the world in order to uphold our conditioning and protect our comfort zones. This undermines all progress. When individuals do not take responsibility for their inner worldview, they fail to act in harmony with the natural order of the universe. Changing the world has become a personal mind game within each individual, of seeking to impose one's personal will on others in order to accommodate one's own agenda, a problem discussed at length in *The Science and Practice of Humility*.

A common misconception is that in order to change the world, we must change its external appearance while allowing our own inner demons to continue running amok. This mistaken approach will continue to drive nails into the coffin of humanity until we learn that in order to change the world, we must first change ourselves. The evolution of our species does not depend on a new socioeconomic system. It depends entirely on a new internal terrain. This may be difficult for most of us, because we have never been taught to acknowledge and face our own internal demons, but if we are sincere in the wish to understand ourselves and our place in the universe, then the science of humility will show the one and only way. Only a select few have been capable of fully assimilating the science of humility, but these revered masters and sages can lead the rest of us with the light and love of their supreme accomplishment. Their lucid insight into that great mystery that shimmers beyond words and action will wear away the hard ignorance of the world in the same way that water slowly but surely wears away the hardest rock. To the ascended masters and sages, humility is an ever-moving vehicle that carries the individual unerringly to the full realization of enlightened awareness, illuminating the whole world like the sun in a cloudless sky.

The Science and Practice of Humility provides the reader with a clear understanding of what spiritual evolution and illumined consciousness really mean. When fully comprehended the science of humility can inspire the real change within the heart and mind of each individual that is required to bring about real change in the world we all share.

1
The Great Work of Eternity

*T*he great work of eternity is the common truth and way within the universe. It is that indestructible work that leads an individual to the science of humility. Liberation rests upon the total understanding of consciousness and the reality we experience. In the deepest chamber of esoteric knowledge within the wisdom traditions, it is an eternal truth that consciousness exists on three planes: physical, mental, and spiritual. These three planes of consciousness are the foundation of the totality of our being. To truly "know thyself" is to know how these three planes dwell within and how they are impressed from without.

FEAR IS OUR FRIEND

Throughout the journey of eternity, many beings within the universe have attained a state of consciousness that leads them to an untouchable freedom. Even as the chaos of the universe continues, many individuals continue to share the knowledge and wisdom of eternity with the masses. One of the great mysteries of life is that many have brought this wisdom forth on an individual level, yet collectively we have not assimilated this eternal knowledge. We have had the knowledge of eternal freedom for eons of time, yet in a great span of evolution, only a select few have realized its truth.

The main reason for this conundrum is that most individuals try to ignore the darker parts of their being. However, not one aspect of our life can be ignored; that would imply that we are not part of the greater whole. One of the great errors passed down from certain teachers of eternity results from the teaching that, as human beings, we are born into ignorance. Many teachers suggest that we ignore that part of our being and instead focus on our Eternal Self. This nurtures an arrogant positivity in opposition to the conditioned ego within our own being. All this does is cause neurosis within seekers of truth: they are taught that their life has been under the spell of the conditioned ego, which proves that their life has been lived in ignorance, but the antidote suggested is to practice ignorance again with a fake positivity that cannot and will not last. Focusing on positivity erroneously implies that negativity does not exist. Our ego cannot be understood by ignoring the reality that it is part of our being.

In contrast, those who have reached enlightenment have delved into all aspects of their being to find freedom hiding within the dark shadows. As they ascend to higher and higher states of consciousness, they see that the parasite of our being known as the ego cannot be ignored. It is only by embracing their own full being that they reach a true and authentic liberation, which is the true essence of those states of consciousness referred to in the wisdom traditions as *moksha, nirvana, nirvikalpa samadhi, samadhi, satori,* and many others. Key to this possibility is correcting our distorted perception of the two key emotional virtues or polarities of our being: fear and love. One of the gravest mistakes of numerous spiritual doctrines is the idea that the way to destroy fear in oneself is to just ignore it and focus on love. But that is not an authentic love, and such a process will result in the internal annihilation of the being. That raises the question, "Isn't everything love?" The answer is "yes," but if we just cling to that idea without investigating our own inner world, we will only be reacting via the ego, and then love is limited by boundaries attuned to our own likes or dislikes. If we go that route, we will always have a tough time coming to grips with the reality that our love is actually inauthentic and guided by fear.

Exploring the fear that resides within the dark regions of our being leads us to where love for all life is born. But this does not mean that we should manipulate life, such as can happen when we recognize that fear at its core is an illusion, along with believing that *illusion* is a dirty word. Then the ego is still directing our reality, which in itself is an illusion of the psyche. But *illusion* is not a dirty word; it is part of our being, thus to ignore the illusionary side of our nature is to ignore certain key parts of our inner and outer world.

If we take a close look at our relationship with fear and engage in a deep introspection into consciousness, we will find that fear is actually one of our closest friends. That may be a bitter pill to swallow for some. Building an understanding of fear as a friend may appear paradoxical, yet it is a necessary truth. For fear serves to teach us about certain parts of our inner nature. In a sense the ego is fundamentally flawed: designed into the egotistical side of our psyche where fear resides is a natural impulse to escape the clutches of separation, which is the grand illusion. So fear, when seen with greater clarity, is actually a guiding principle of human consciousness.

As our friend fear constantly humbles us, which leads ultimately to more expansive states of consciousness. Fear guides us to our natural state of humility. Throughout the ages many beings have gained an intellectual understanding of humility, which they use to judge others in the false belief that they have reached the gates of heaven or that they see through the eyes of God. Fear will continue to humble those with such fallacious beliefs, until they finally see the science that lies at the core of humility. The science of humility can only be comprehended by those who have been humbled so completely by fear that they let go of life to the utmost degree, thus allowing a trust of the universe to be born.

Trust is the real driving force of evolution or we could say growth in consciousness. Throughout the ages this scientific foundation of humility has been misconstrued by those who falsely believe that to have complete trust in the universal unfoldment is a passive approach to life and a sign of weakness. Those who believe this are suggesting that they are outside of the universe and consciousness, thus they are swimming against evolution. This is a good indication why only a small minority of beings have embodied the eternal wisdom and the collective has not: fear and humility have not been felt in their truest sense, as natural pathways to the evolution of consciousness. Those who have the arrogant attitude that humility is weakness will never know the totality of their being.

THE MOST POWERFUL FORCE
IS PARADOXICAL

Within one of the treatises of eternity, known as the *Tao Te Ching*, written by the holy sage Lao-tzu of China, we can see into the deeper more subtle science of humility and how it dispels the illusion that humility is weakness for those with the intuition to see. Chapter 78 reads:

> *Nothing in the world*
> *is as soft and yielding as water.*
> *Yet for dissolving the hard and inflexible,*
> *nothing can surpass it.*
> *The soft overcomes the hard;*
> *the gentle overcomes the rigid.*
> *Everyone knows this is true,*
> *but few can put it into practice.*
> *Therefore the Master remains*
> *serene in the midst of sorrow.*
> *Evil cannot enter his heart.*
> *Because he has given up helping,*
> *he is people's greatest help.*
> *True words seem paradoxical.*[1]

One who has explored fear will explain to you that indeed humility is the deepest most mysterious science and that there are no words to describe it. But our intuition can be ignited by exploration of the occult properties behind humility. For example, the elemental principle of humility is water and the gender principle is the feminine. The element of water is found within all life-forms.

It is what gives nourishment to life on a planetary body, where it maintains the health and growth of all existence. As the *Tao Te Ching* mentions, water is that which overcomes the hard, as water wears away at a rock over time. The softness of water is incomparable, but in its humble nature it is paradoxically the most powerful force of nature. We human beings are predominately water.

The feminine principle of the universe is receptive. This receptivity is the motherly nature that all beings possess, which nourishes and maintains the growth of consciousness. Just as water allows a tree to flourish physically, the receptive nature of the universe allows the consciousness of an individual to expand. When these are truthfully understood, then deeper and more profound insights into our being and its relationship to the universe are comprehended. Humility has a mysterious quality, which transforms the consciousness into a greater perception of the whole rather than getting caught in the detail of worldly affairs. This is one of the distinct differences between those with less knowledge and those who know the science of humility.

THE REAL NATURE OF EVOLUTION

One of the staggering errors of consciousness is that, having been drawn into the chaos of the universe, we egotistically believe that we are self-righteous enough to know what is best for others; we engage in manipulating others into our version of reality. This is one of the main symptoms of the destruction of consciousness, which in some wisdom traditions is referred to as "devolution."

On the other hand, when we experience life through humility, we gain the ability to embrace higher and more profound insights into the universe. For example, when we look into the cellular world through a microscope, we find a group of cells in chaos, but as we continue to zoom out we see greater expressions of harmony or order until we reach a community of cells that make up a sentient being. When more clarity is gained with a view from above, an amazing harmony and a symbiotic symphony of life are revealed. The science of humility or true and authentic humility can only be experienced when we are lifted out of the daily mundane dramas of everyday existence by such a vision: that on one level there is the chaos of life, yet on a higher plane, all of this chaos is actually in a rhythmic harmony. This vision is what evolves the individual and creation itself, as the individual is a reflection of the cosmos.

This truth is taught by the wisdom traditions of eternity, which speak of the individual as the microcosm of the universe, such as in the second of the seven universal laws expounded by Hermes Trismegistus, known as "the scribe of Gods" in ancient Egypt and Greece (who was in fact the Egyptian God Thoth). He presented these "Hermetic Principles" as the foundation of the universe. The second states:

II. The Principle of Correspondence
As above, so below; as below, so above.[2]

The evolution of the individual as a natural process within the evolution of the universe has been intellectualized and hijacked by the collective ego for many ages of time. The universe is eternal and always expanding, and so is the consciousness at the foundation of the universe. The individual is a focal point of that universal consciousness when the science of humility has come through that focal point. Far too often the experiential aspect of life is discounted, with preference given to a more intellectual comprehension of matter and the external world. The inherent problem with such an approach is that it denies that a world exists within each individual. In the modern era science is erroneously perceived as properly pertaining only to an investigation of matter and external space.

This perception is supported by the false belief that the external world is all that exists. Throughout the planet most of our socially accepted institutions have been built around this grand delusion, which breeds ignorance of our inner world. As a result the experiences of others are judged based on the misconception that we have reached the pinnacle in evolution and that an individual's consciousness cannot reach higher states of awareness. In fact, consciousness is always in a state of growth when the individual is in harmony with the universe. So the idea that we can judge another's experience is inconsistent with the very fabric of consciousness. As one treatise of eternity known as the *Srimad Bhagavatam* reads:

> You are always expanding your internal potency, and therefore no one can understand you. Learned scientists and learned scholars can examine the atomic constitution of the material world or even the planets, but still they are unable to calculate your energy and potency, although you are present before them.[3]

This profound wisdom explains why the science of humility, the totality of a being, and evolution itself have not been understood by the majority of the world. This can be corrected by gaining a clear understanding of the true nature of the great work of eternity. This work has nothing to do with performing acts or good deeds in the external world. The great work of eternity is the beginning of sincere self-work, which means to look within so completely that that becomes your mode of consciousness. Everything experienced "without" is examined in the light of your own introspection, without exception. Looking so deeply within naturally brings an end to judgments of others. The gateways of eternal knowledge begin to open.

Throughout the ages the great work of eternity has been misinterpreted because of the ignorance that blinds us to seeing that the individual is an integral part of the universe. As a result nature and the universe have been regarded something to conquer rather than something to live in harmony with. The distorted belief that work is only done "outside" the individual, has led to the idea that this is what molds the individual or, even more absurd, the universe, as if the universe needs to be helped along in its evolution. Nothing could be more ridiculous than the belief that we are the architects of the Earth and universe.

Evolution is not the progress made in the external world, even though in some cases that may be the outcome. Evolution begins only when the individual seeks to find the source of all life within their own being. Sincere introspection reveals that true evolution is the natural expansion of consciousness, which in fact is a reflection of the eternal universe. The gravest error among sentient beings is the association of evolution with the development of the material world, along with being ignorant about the consciousness that gives birth to the material world. As this great error is revealed from within, we come to know that only consciousness evolves. As true evolution is the evolution of consciousness, then understanding the totality of our being is to be able to comprehend all facets of consciousness. This is the key to individual and collective liberation on all planes of existence. Still, this does not mean that we disregard the material or physical world, as it is an aspect of consciousness and a major part of our being. To associate consciousness with only the mental state of a being is a fallacious attempt to understand the being and the universe we live in.

We enslave ourselves by accepting the illusion that the source of the universe and the great work of eternity are found outside of our consciousness. This includes the socially accepted slavery of transactions to obtain what we call money. Seeing the world as being only external keeps the individual in a dishonest state with an attitude of doing business with everybody. Here *business* means bartering or seeking to gain something from someone either physically, mentally, or spiritually to boost one's own individuality over others. This takes place even with those who individuals falsely believe they love, but typically only possess as material attachments. The love that exists within this mode of consciousness is not true love, because it is bound by the limitations of one's judgments. This false love is a symptom of the illusion that the great work of eternity is in the external world.

The social acceptance of this form of slavery arises from the distortion of the great work of eternity, because we believe the source of all power is outside ourselves, as if the universe is working against us rather than just happening to us or working with us. When this is the reality of our consciousness, then suffering will continue to be part of our life, because we are seeking freedom or salvation through emotional and material comforts, which in the end are momentary. True freedom from all forms of slavery—physical, mental, or spiritual—begins with a sincere quest to the depths of the great work of eternity.

THE IRREDUCIBLE ESSENCE

The final goal of the great work of eternity is to truly know and live in harmony with that mystery known within the wisdom traditions of eternity as Tao, Brahman, Sunya or Void, Allah, God, Infinity, Universe, and by many other names. They all refer to the same irreducible essence of the universe, the ground of consciousness that many institutions aspire to know more of, but inherently fall short of. Religion, science, philosophy, psychology, and numerous others are desperately searching for an intellectual understanding of what that mysterious essence is.

Central to all of the wisdom traditions is the teaching that one who knows the essence, knows once and for all what liberation is. This state of liberation is isolated to a sage who knows the essence not as something apart from them, but as them. The difficulty for most who are trying to reach the liberated state is that they are after an intellectual discovery that is pleasing to their conditioning. The unfoldment of the great work of eternity is to reveal the liberation from within as a direct experience. It is not about filling oneself full of the noise of conventional knowledge. The science of humility is beyond words; it is the expression of that irreducible essence found within all wisdom traditions.

The various references to the universal essence, such as Tao or Brahman or Void, all point to an underlying field of forces where everything happens in a vast inclusive space. Now modern science has astonishingly agreed in no uncertain terms with the wisdom traditions of antiquity by revealing that there is a chaotic field of forces underlying all matter, which is beyond the scope of intellectual reasoning, beyond beliefs and ideologies. But throughout the ages this knowledge has been conceptualized as a God who or which created the universe and condemns those who don't believe in "it." This concept assumes that God is insecure and has a big ego to protect by accumulating blind followers. Nothing could be more ridiculous and further from the truth. We have come to such erroneous conclusions because we are trying to understand from an intellectual standpoint of a conditioned individual.

As we go further in our explorations, we will discover in more detail how a conclusive understanding of the universal essence may be unattainable from an intellectual standpoint. God in the realm of speech is a concept, yet what the concept refers to is the field of forces within the Void, not some Being lording it over the individual and the world. All descriptions of the universal essence point to the same source: the field of forces within and coming out of vast empty space. The great work of eternity is the process an individual goes through in gaining more wisdom of how the irreducible essence of the universe is expressed through the framework of three planes of consciousness—physical, mental, and spiritual—which allows a harmonic pattern to exist in reality. Rather than intellectualizing about what that harmonic pattern may be, the science of humility gives us the ability to know it as a direct experience, to nurture the possibility that all beings might once and for all be completely free.

2

The Physical Canvas

ven though the knowledge that the physical world, along with the mental and spiritual worlds, is itself consciousness has been lost throughout the ages, it has stayed alive within the wisdom traditions of eternity. But this will only be revealed to those who are sincere in exploring the great work of eternity. As this knowledge is eternal, it cannot be studied with a common scientific approach, as the majority of sciences only investigate finite matters. No external science can ever reach the depths of the eternal or explain the experiencer of that.

The way we as individuals experience reality is as if everything is impressed on us from without. Thus we develop an "us against the universe" or "us against them" mentality. This leads to the belief that we are separate from the universe, a universal error, from which we gain the sense that the physical world is either going to conquer us or be conquered by us. This molds the psyche into a schizophrenic conflict of attempting to lord it over nature.

Part of our ignorance arises from our thinking that our way

of constructing things, from the outside to the inside, applies to nature. Nature is falsely thought to be something created in a step-by-step process. The wisdom traditions know it is absurd to think this way, because all forms of nature are grown from the inside to outside. For example, when we see a flower blossom, it has not been put together in a bit-by-bit process; on the contrary, all of the flower's parts move as one from the center. Babies are grown like this too. Similarly, consciousness expands as its three planes.

The expansion of wisdom will take us from the illusion of a constructed world and into alignment with the harmonic resonance of the universe. The wisdom traditions teach that once we embark on the great work of eternity, we will find that not only can we live in harmony with the universe on a mental and spiritual plane, but also that we need to live in harmony with the physical plane as well. One of the resulting insights into consciousness is that even though individuals appear separate from all life in the physical plane, we are more intrinsically interwoven into the fabric of matter than we can imagine. In this pure seeing we can gain knowledge that we are not only an integral part of the cosmos, but are in truth the eyes and the ears of the cosmos and planet Earth.

ORGANIC LIFE HARMONICS

A common misconception is that Earth is nothing more than a solid mass floating through space. As this falsity is engrained in the collective psyche, we have forged an idea that the universe (and all matters that pertain to the physical world) is nothing more than a random event or accident. When we look into the physical plane, it may appear random, but delving more deeply into the facts reveals that consciousness is the foundation of the universe. The physical plane is the outer garment of the mental and spiritual planes of consciousness.

There is nothing random about the universe and Earth. Earth is a living organism with complete awareness of itself. All celestial bodies throughout the universe are not only spectacular physical organisms, but are highly spiritual beings, which is hard for the human species to fathom. Being able to understand the consciousness of a planet is tantamount to comprehending the function and purpose of the entire universe.

From the human perspective, we belong to and are part of Earth, but we are not Earth in its entirety. In some cases it may appear that the human species does not belong to Earth, because we so often act against nature, like a cancer. But humans are natural to Earth. This can be seen in the way the energies of Earth work through us to maintain the planet's own growth. According to the wisdom traditions of eternity, this planetary energy builds a structure, which is esoterically known as the "General Law." One of the teachers of eternity known as Boris Mouravieff explained this General Law within the treatise of eternity *Gnosis: Study and Commentaries on the Esoteric Tradition of Eastern Orthodoxy— Book One—Exoteric Cycle*:

As a cell of humanity, man forms part of organic life on Earth. This life in its ensemble represents a very sensitive organ of our planet, playing an important role in the economy of our solar system. As a cell of this organ, man finds himself under the influence of the *General Law*, which keeps him in his place. In fact, this law leaves him a certain margin or tolerance. It allows him some *free movement* within the limits it sets. Within these boundaries, which are very limited objectively although subjectively they appear vast, man can give free rein to his fantasies and his ambitions.

Without going too far into the definition of these limits and detailed description of the components of this *General Law*, we can say as an example that one of those factors is hunger: the servitude of working to assure our subsistence. The chain: sexual instinct; procreation; and the care of parents for their children, is another factor. The esoteric maxim that applies to this aspect of life is conceived thus: *carnal love is necessary for the general good.*[1]

The General Law is Earth's constitution, which all organic life abides by. Human beings are an integral part of organic life on Earth especially when we live in harmony with the General Law. Living a simple life in accordance with Earth's laws gives us an enormous opportunity to discover the great work of eternity and gain a universal perception of the General Law. But throughout the ages a collective parasite has infected the profane,* leading to outlandish beliefs such as only finding significance in outward appearances and taking the illusion of carnal love for real love. Even though carnal love maintains human life on Earth, it is also our closest tie back to the animal kingdom. Believing that our animal drives are love suppresses the evolution of consciousness. Love is limitless, and true love has nothing to do with sexual desire.

The human being is the most sensitive organism on this planet, which gives us the ability to contribute to its stewardship or its destruction. Because we do not see we are part of Earth, we

---

*Chapter 5 presents two contrasting states of consciousness, one associated with a sage; the other is the state of consciousness of the ego that is caught in details; it is this that is referred to as "the masses" or "the profane."

choose to challenge it and insult its conscious intelligence. We have developed an inner psychic disease known as the "ego." The ego is a manufactured mental program that operates within most sentient beings. It is this program running within all beings that keeps the physical plane in a state of chaos, because most beings only see their part on the planet in a narrow form rather than seeing themselves as an integral part of a grand planetary unfoldment. In fact, the ego is the ultimate extension of a planetary system's sensitivity.

The parasite known as the ego will always try to get us to believe that we have reached our pinnacle in evolution, because the ego cannot see that the universe is constantly unfolding. This false belief enslaves us. From an enlightened perspective, it is clear that everything on the physical plane is in a state of unfoldment, all the way from a cell to the universe. But one who is caught in the detail of life does not see this unfoldment. When we can visualize the great unfoldment in our own lives and extended out into the universe, we will begin to see and feel a harmony that has its own intelligence, one that is beyond the normal realm of thought.

UNIVERSAL HARMONICS

The harmony we speak of exists everywhere. One with less knowledge will continue to see chaos, but one who has dived into the great work of eternity will see and feel something beyond words.

Within the universe two cosmic principles, energies, or forces underlie matter. In the wisdom traditions these two forces are known by many different expressions, such as: masculine and feminine, solar and lunar, Heaven and Earth, creative and receptive, attraction and repulsion, active and passive, and positive and negative. In Hinduism they are known in Sanskrit as Shiva and Shakti, in Taoism they are known in Chinese as yang and yin, and in relation to the subtle body in mysticism, these principles are known as *pingala* and *ida* in Sanskrit. This hidden principle is found in the esoteric wisdom of Christianity through the representation of Adam and Eve as the cosmic energies. As a foundational building block of reality, these two cosmic principles are expressed by the universal laws that were expounded by such teachers of eternity as Hermes Trismegistus. His seventh great law reads:

VII. The Principle of Gender
Gender is in everything; everything has its
Masculine and Feminine Principles;
Gender manifests on all planes.[2]

This universal law manifests on all three planes of consciousness. These two forces are symbolized in the physical world as male and female; the two manifest through sex on the physical plane, as a child is born from this union. On the higher planes these two energies manifest in a more subtle and profound way. This perpetual dance of duality is part of the structure of the universe on the physical plane, whether as male and female or galactic formations.

This duality built into the fabric of reality from the microcosm to the macrocosm is synchronized through orbital systems. These orbital structures exist in various modalities from the binary system of our sun and its unseen opposite, to the more traditional cyclical orbits of planets around a central star. There may be other orbital systems within the universe that could be hard for us to fathom. But there is one common theme among all orbital systems: they all move around a central point. In the physical plane the universal design is inherently the same, from a cell to a galaxy.

Galaxies are involved in a monumental orbit around a center point of the universe. This central point is the source of all creation, the foundation from where all three planes of consciousness were born. The ancient wisdom of India explains that this is where the "breath of Brahma" originates; it is also referred to as the "eye of Brahma," which can be seen as a reflection of the physical eye of the human being.

The eye of Brahma is the great Void or nothingness where everything originates. Chapter 1 of the *Tao Te Ching* offers a profound contemplation into this mystery of the unmanifest grand center.

> *The tao that can be told*
> *is not the eternal Tao.*
> *The name that can be named*
> *is not the eternal Name.*
> *The unnamable is the eternally real.*
> *Naming is the origin*
> *of all particular things.*
> *Free from desire, you realize the mystery.*
> *Caught in desire, you see only the manifestations.*
> *Yet mystery and manifestations*
> *arise from the same source.*
> *This source is called darkness.*
> *Darkness within darkness.*
> *The gateway to all understanding.*[3]

Figure 2.1. Sri Yantra mandala

While all galaxies orbit around this grand center, suggesting how long one of these orbits would take would be highly speculative. In the grand scheme of the eternal universe, our Milky Way has probably never reached one full rotation around the center; such is the incomprehensible size of the universe. But if we could see the totality of the universe, there would be innumerable galaxies in their own particular orbits forming a cosmic pattern around the grand center. The magnitude of this divine harmony is beyond our intellectual understanding. The best way that this universal form could be symbolized is through an artist's expression of a sacred mandala, with life emanating from a central point in a fractal manner, forming a sacred pattern in perfect harmony (see figure 2.1).

GALACTIC HARMONICS

Galaxies exist within the space of the universe. They are a gravitationally bound system made up of stars, stellar remnants, an interstellar medium of gas and dust, dark matter, and numerous planets, star systems, star clusters, and moons surrounded by a sparse interstellar medium of gas, dust, and cosmic rays. A galaxy has its beginning and ensuing formation in what we would deem a major celestial event. When a galaxy is born it undergoes a slow process of formation in which it achieves higher and higher states of vibration. The higher vibratory structure of an ascending galaxy is beyond intellectual understanding. The only way we could contemplate this is by seeing how galactic formation and evolution are mirrored in our own being. As Hermes Trismegistus explained, "As above, so below; as below, so above." We realize this again through the harmony of the universe that grows the structure.

As the structure of a galaxy grows over eons, more and more stars, planets, and moons come into manifestation. As the transformation of a galaxy reaches higher expressions, it forms a harmonized elliptical or spiral shape, which rotates and ebbs and flows in and around its own cosmic center. In a spiral galaxy such as our own Milky Way, all of the stars, planets, and moons follow the pattern within the galaxy, as they are intrinsic parts of the spiral's shape. They travel to the furthest point of the galaxy and then make their return to the cosmic center while following the rotation of the galaxy.

At every level we find a mirror of that which is above: just as galaxies orbit the center of the universe, innumerable systems of planets within a galaxy orbit around its center. If we look into our solar system, we see that our planets are in their own orbits around the central sun. All planets vary in the time it takes to complete one orbit, which could tempt an observer to believe our solar system is in perpetual chaos. Yet from the Milky Way's perspective, our solar system is in the very same divine harmony as that which makes up the galaxies orbiting around the birthplace of the universe. Likewise the Milky Way has a central point that gave birth to all celestial bodies within it. This galactic center is made up of a quantity of photons so immense that if we were to see it with our naked eye, our eyes would be burnt right out of our heads. The wisdom traditions of eternity explain that if our solar system were to pass through the Milky Way's photonic center, all three planes of consciousness would be transformed so dramatically that, once out the other side, it would be almost impossible for the new consciousness to believe it was the former. Even the physical plane would be transformed to a slight degree, which is hard to imagine.

Just as a tree's seed holds the image of the tree's structure within it, the physical image of a spiral formation with a central point of power is held within the cosmic seed of the universe. All seeds in fact carry within them an electromagnetic signature that maintains the structure of the universe, which again brings us back to the law of correspondence. The Milky Way—and all galaxies—function the same way as the universe; looking into the structure of a galaxy, we would see the same harmony playing out on a different scale, with an incalculable number of solar systems functioning in the same harmony as the universe and galaxies. However, from an unenlightened perspective, one that was looking too close into the detail, the Milky Way would appear to be in constant chaos.

PLANETARY HARMONICS

Imagine we were a civilization living on the moon. We would look out every day and see this beautiful glowing blue and green planet in perfect harmony with the sun, moon, and the other planets of the solar system. A similar harmony is found on all planets within the cosmos, especially those with organic life. The problem with most planets in the universe is that the beings with an awareness of the planet they inhabit do not see it this way, due to their ignorance of the great work of eternity.

Yet one whose perception is attuned to the great work of eternity can see that their planet is a mirror reflection of the galaxy and universe. From this enlightened perspective, the Milky Way and the universe can be seen within the structure of each planet. Our Earth consists of three primary layers known as the crust, mantle, and core. These primary layers are made up of six secondary layers, which include the atmosphere, crust, upper mantle, lower mantle, outer core, and inner core. All life exists on the surface, the crust of the planet. Beneath it are the upper and lower mantle. Even deeper is the layer known as the outer core and within it is the center known as the inner core. The inner core is a molten iron ball of immense heat, around which all the outer layers rotate in a fashion that creates electromagnetism; this is how the magnetic fields of Earth are born. If the rotation of the layers within Earth ceased, then the magnetic field would break down, the atmosphere would disintegrate, and—even though this is hard to fathom—we would float off into space. Fortunately, Earth, like all planets, has a central point round which all life orbits.

HUMAN HARMONICS

The pattern found within the universe, galaxies, and planets is not just bound to these high physical/spiritual beings of great complexity. The pattern also unfolds within the organic life of any planet, especially within sentient beings that have an awareness of themselves. The most sensitive organism of Earth, known as the human being, is where this pattern blossoms most beautifully, yet it is a mystery found by few. The human body is the host of trillions of cells that make up billions of communities. When seen from a distance, these cells have their own orbital patterns; together they create an amazing harmony around the central point of the human, which we call the heart.

The heart, like the inner core of a planet, has an electromagnetic current that nourishes all organs and cells. This current stabilizes and harmonizes the inner world of biology, but if the heart is disturbed, then the whole inner world suffers. A lot of the disturbance within the human instrument is because of the organ within the body known as the brain. The human brain is where the intangible world of mind is born. The brain is a governing apparatus that is supposed to work in unison with the kingdom of the heart, but what happens in most cases is that—because of its governing role in the being—the brain believes it is king and brings trouble to the current of the heart. The symptom of conflict can be seen when we believe we are our thoughts rather than living an intuitive existence, open to whatever the universe has in store for us. This is the result of getting caught up in the details or, put another way, the storm of thoughts and emotions. If we can step back and know first and foremost that we are the heart because that is the center, then we can keep our inner being in harmony.

The brain and the heart are actually both electromagnetic signatures of the true heart of consciousness, or center point, which is a reflection of the universal grand center, with which there is always a harmony resonating on all levels of the universe.

INTELLIGENT HARMONICS

The origin of the universal harmony is hard for those who only live on the physical plane to comprehend, because to find the source of this phenomenon, we have to contemplate deeply. The essence behind harmony on the physical plane is an intelligence that creates both the chaos and the order within the world of manifestation. This intelligence holds everything in place, yet follows a path of evolution.

The easiest way to find and demonstrate this intelligence is through the human body. We never question why our body operates the way it does. For example, do you truly know how you open and close your hand? Is there a process to learn or manual to follow? We never have to learn how to open and close our hand because we can just do it. An electrical current or signal is sent from the brain to the hand instantaneously to create the motion of opening and closing. This is the same with all functions of the body, which all respond to a signal coming from the brain. Our bodies are actually doing an infinite number of things at once without our having to think about them.

The electrical signal is the very intelligence we are speaking of. It is so primal that dwelling on it will open up gateways of eternal knowledge. The intelligence that opens and closes your hand is the same as that which forms a spiral of a galaxy. What does this say for the intelligence? Do you control the intelligence or does it control you unconsciously? The truth is that we are not conscious of the intelligence within the body because most functions within the physical instrument are accomplished without our conscious attention. The digestion of food, for example, or the operation of the cellular world when we blink our eyes, all happen beyond our awareness. All of these functions of the body are in perfect harmony without our conscious participation. Even if we become more aware of them, we will never have full awareness of all functions and patterns of the body. The unnamable intelligence that maintains the harmony of the universe manifests through the unconscious.

This offers us a profound insight: without forcing ourselves on life, we discover life in perfect harmony. This is taught in the Taoist philosophy of *wu-wei,* which illustrates the universal art of "non-doing" or, in other words, "not forcing." In receiving intelligence rather than trying to control it, a sacred harmony is produced all the way from a cell to the universe. The universe, galaxies, stars, moons, and planetary systems all embody the science of humility, thus the divine patterns of eternity are manifested through that sacred science. The science of humility and the intelligence we are speaking of can in fact never be truly understood from the physical plane of consciousness, because both emanate out of the grand center of the universe, which is beyond the manifest world. In order to know the totality of our existence, we need to know more about the central point of the three planes of consciousness, which is a mirror reflection of the grand center. The Oracle of Delphi once said, "Man, know thyself, and thou shalt know the universe and its Gods!"[4]

To truly engage in the great work of eternity, we need to understand the power this intelligence has over the physical plane. Greater understanding of this intelligence can be found through exploration of the mental plane of consciousness, because the physical and mental planes are intimately mingled with each other. The physical plane is the covering of the mental world.

3
The Mental Calligraphy

🙗

*T*he harmony and intelligence playing out in the physical
world are reflected in the harmony and intelligence functioning in the subatomic world. Amazingly, the subatomic particles within an atom, such as electrons, neutrons, and protons,
function in the same way as galaxies, planets, humans, cells, and
so on. Electrons have their own orbits around a central point
within an atom. When looked at in too much detail, the subatomic world appears chaotic, yet when we take a step back we
see the exact same harmony as we discover with galactic bodies.
The unnamable intelligence not only functions in the world we
see, but also exists in the one we can't see.

Many of the problems of most beings throughout the cosmos arise from the lack of knowledge about how the subatomic
world is connected to our thoughts and emotions. Subatomic
particles are controlled by the mental plane of consciousness,
which creates the physical world. We create the reality we experience, every moment of it, but throughout eternity we have not

truthfully understood this. This natural creative ability has often been viewed in a distorted way. The ego distracts the individual by focusing on an inauthentic "love and light" attitude, with the goal of experiencing only a pleasant reality. But experiencing a pleasant reality is never achieved with such an attitude toward life, because ignoring the darker aspects of our being creates a situation of disruption. The result of ignorance within our being is that the subatomic world we create manifests as the physical world in a perpetual state of war. This stimulates a deep fear of all life, which maintains the illusion of separation. War is nothing more than a symptom of an individual's conditioned psyche projected into the physical plane. Individuals who believe they are creating their own reality by just focusing on love and light while ignoring other aspects of their being are only in truth contributing to chaos and entropy.

One who is sincere in exploring the mental plane will realize that the harmony that exists at all levels from an electron to a galaxy can only be embodied by those who are capable of sensing their center and intuitively knowing the inner harmony and intelligence. Then and only then can we truly create our own reality because we are moving into the center that is the source of all creation that includes all three planes of consciousness.

MENTAL ALCHEMY

The wisdom traditions of eternity know we create our own reality. At the same time they understand we can only truly know this if we comprehend the totality of our being. Focusing their energy on the mental plane toward conscious manifestation, they created an ancient science known as "mental alchemy." This was a key subject in the mystery schools of Sumer, Babylon, Chaldea, and Egypt, where neophytes were taught the relationship between the physical and mental planes. Study of the properties of electro-magnetism gave them the insight that the physical plane is the opposite magnetic pole of the mental plane, which gives rise to a dynamism known in occult terminology as mind-force. The teachers of eternity knew the influence mind-force has over the subatomic world. Alchemy is the science of turning metal into gold, while mental alchemy is the science of turning mental thoughts into golden projections upon the physical world or, in other words, turning the lead of the ego into gold. The mind is like a paint brush and the world we see is our canvas. Mental alchemy is the art of manifestation, which is not as simple as thinking glorious thoughts.

Throughout the ages these teachings have given rise to the illusion that we can create our own reality by just focusing on what we want. That is only an attempt to gain something in the material world to boost and perpetuate the ego. It maintains the illusion of separation. A mental projection coming from the ego won't be what we truly want or need. Such delusions will not result in the manifestation of our conscious projections. In such a case attention will not be focused in one place, and there will be no force behind it to become a reality. Those who attempt to create their own reality from the egotistical side of their psyche are no better than those who are not aware that they create their own reality. Both are contributing to a collective projection of chaos and entropy because their mental states are not focused in one direction. Destruction of organic life is the result.

Such individuals—who still live within the prison of the ego—will never be granted access into the great work of eternity because they do not know the absolute truth of unity. Mental alchemy has nothing to do with being better than others nor has it anything to do with creating a pleasant situation for oneself. The true art of mental alchemy takes place when you discover something that is natural to your inner being through the process of exploring your own consciousness to find out more about who you are. Then your energy will naturally flow toward that passion and then your art will be expressed on the physical plane—hence you create your own reality. One of the main goals in mental alchemy is exactly this discovery of one's purpose, which leads one down the path toward deeper realization of the true self that unfolds like a flower.

DHARMA

An individual's life purpose or mission is known as *dharma* in Sanskrit or *te* in Chinese. *Dharma* is a word that is not easily translated; it describes the path of life that is only experienced by one with an evolved consciousness. Some definitions of dharma are "a law," or "function," or the Buddhist doctrine or method. We could say that dharma is a fundamental order or pattern of the universe brought through an individual's consciousness. One of the teachers of eternity, Swami Sri Yukteswar, explained dharma in its truest sense as being the "mental virtue" of an enlightened individual or a characteristic of a coming age. He revealed that as we go through what the Hindus call the *yugas* in Sanskrit (cycles of time/consciousness), the dharma within a being becomes so refined that eventually the individual will not just have a feeling of what God or the universe is, but an intellectual understanding of the Absolute. One of the treatises of eternity known as

The Holy Science, which was intuitively written by Swami Sri Yukteswar, states:

> The sun also has another motion by which it revolves round a grand center called *Vishnunabhi,* which is the seat of the creative power, *Brahma,* the universal magnetism. *Brahma* regulates *dharma,* the mental virtue of the internal world.
>
> When the sun in its revolution round its dual comes to the place nearest to this grand center, the seat of *Brahma* (an event which takes place when the Autumnal Equinox comes to the first point of Aries), *dharma,* the mental virtue, becomes so much developed that man can easily comprehend all, even the mysteries of spirit.[1]

The art of mental alchemy and the dharma path go hand in hand; they are the divine attributes on the journey to enlightenment. They are the electromagnetic signatures of the great work of eternity, which ultimately leads the initiate into the science of humility. Both the art and virtue of these divination tools are experiential, difficult to describe in words to another who is not having the experience. Those who have never touched the great work of eternity will never understand; they will condemn these virtues because they are ignorant of themselves. In the wisdom traditions only those who had begun the process of letting go of the rigid false ego were accepted into the mystery schools. Those who are sincere in exploring the depths of their own being and can see their ego fading in the distance will be able to let these divine virtues shine forth. That will allow them to truly create their own reality.

However, we do face a few roadblocks on the path of creating our own reality. We cannot alter the structure of the universe, such as by changing the constitution of the seven universal laws, or the physical appearance of Earth. Also, the conscious creations of one who is not empty or pure enough will always be impeded by another's *prarabdha karma* (personal karma). We create our experience through the people we meet in the events of life and the dharma we follow. We mentally project situations, which create events; we can choose to be aware of these crossroads or remain ignorant. Life is thus a sequence of synchronicities, not coincidences.

MENTAL TRANSMUTATION

The core teaching within mental alchemy, known as "mental transmutation," is the art and knowledge of how to transform the conditions of the universe through the microcosm of a human being. In a treatise of eternity known as *The Kybalion,* mental transmutation is explained:

> Mind (as well as metals and elements) may be transmuted, from state to state; degree to degree; condition to condition; pole to pole; vibration to vibration. True Hermetic Transmutation is a Mental Art.[2]

So mental transmutation is an experiential art designed by the sincere mental alchemists. One explores the results of mental transmutation through one's own experience. As one goes deeper into this art, it has a profound effect on consciousness because it transforms the individual's perception of reality into seeing the subtle realms behind the physical plane. We have referred to this subtle realm as the subatomic world, which is a scientific term.

What we are really speaking of is the energetic world or world of energy. When we evolve into the mental plane of consciousness and assimilate mental alchemy and transmutation, we discover that the physical plane is made up of subatomic particles, electricity, magnetism, and all other forms of energy.

One who is sincere in the great work of eternity perceives this subtle world of energy. That doesn't mean being able to look into matter, even though this might be the case for some; rather, it means seeing the essence behind whatever physical events are playing out. If we gain this perception of the energetic world, we can begin to contemplate why an event or certain situation has crossed our path. An intuition and a deep knowing begin to grow within, resulting in the ability to read the environment. A deep meditation on the art of mental alchemy or the art of manifesting, brings the realization that the physical world is nothing more than energy, which is driven and molded from the mental plane; thus the mind too is energy.

The physical and mental planes are magnetic opposites that exist under one of the great universal laws. A common bond allows one to flow into the other. Physical matter is condensed energy formed and created by the force of the mind. Teacher of eternity William Walker Atkinson intuitively explains this relationship between the physical and mental planes in correlation to mental alchemy and dharma in his eternal treatise, *Mind Power: The Secret of Mental Magic:*

> The secret of visualization lies in the occult and psychological
> principle that "as is the mental matrix, so is the mental form;
> and as is the mental form, so is the physical materialization." In
> other words, the visualized mental image is the matrix or mould

into which the Mind-Power is poured, and from which it takes form; and around this mental image the deposit of materialization forms—and thus does the ideal become the real. If you wish to get the best effects from Mind-Power you must create a mental image around which the material or physical materialization is formed—and the way to form the proper mental image is by visualization, which thus builds up the matrix or mould in which the Mind-Power pours. And as is the matrix so is the image, and as is the image so is the materialization.[3]

But this can only explain half the picture. Although on an individual level we create our everyday experiences with our mind, yet there are the collective manifestations of the physical world such as a tree, planet, galaxy, and so on. These collective manifestations are blueprints of the universe, but still they are condensed energy. Does the same mind-force that creates our experiences create the whole physical plane? If we associate force with will, then our mind-force—which creates our daily experience—is a mixture of the individual and Divine Will, and the force that creates the blueprint of the universe is the Will of the Divine. (A discussion of Divine Will will come later.) So what truly integrates the physical and mental planes that hold energy in place? What is the force that creates? This force is the universal law that underlies the fabric of both magnetic opposites. It is what we know as vibration.

TRIUNE VIBRATION

Vibration is the third universal law passed down from teacher of eternity Hermes Trismegistus. The third law reads:

III. The Principle of Vibration

Nothing rests; everything moves; everything vibrates.[4]

In the universe everything is in motion, everything is vibration. Matter, energy, mind, thoughts, emotions, and so on are all vibrations. Sound is a good analogy, as sound is vibration. In music the higher the octave, the higher the pitch of sound, which equals a finer vibration. Vibration itself is a musical phenomenon because it ranges in scales. The universe we exist in is a major symphony of cosmic complexity. Creation is vibration in the grandest complexity held together by varying scales of motion. Creation has been symbolized throughout the orient for eons with the ancient symbol *Aum* (OM). This is the primordial sound/vibration of the universe, which is the foundational sound of all mantras. *Aum* (OM) or primordial vibration is the first emanation out of Brahma or the breath of Brahma. The eternal teacher Swami Sri Yukteswar delivers this knowledge with wisdom in the treatise of eternity *The Holy Science* in chapter 1, "The Gospel."

Sutra 3

Parabrahma causes creation, inert Nature (Prakriti), to emerge. From Aum (Pranava, the Word, the manifestation of the Omnipotent Force), come Kala, Time; Desa, Space; and Anu, the Atom (the vibratory structure of creation).

The Word, *Amen* (*Aum*), is the beginning of the Creation. The manifestation of Omnipotent Force (the Repulsion and its complementary expression, Omniscient Feeling or Love, the Attraction) is vibration, which appears as a peculiar sound: the Word, *Amen, Aum*. In its different aspects *Aum* presents the idea of change, which is Time, *Kala*, in the Ever-Unchangeable; and the idea of division, which is Space, *Desa*, in the Ever-Indivisible.[5]

The vibratory structure of creation leads to the illusion of change emanating from the changeless grand center of creation. The vibration that exists within the grand center is that same vibration existing in all sentient beings. The universe is in a musical harmony, yet most beings are not in harmony with it because they are too low in the scale of vibration. If we were attuned to the high tone of creation, we would see the vibration of the physical world and also hear it. An ancient anonymous Hermetic writer once said, "He who understands the Principle of Vibration, has grasped the sceptre of power."[6]

The universal force that creates the motion of vibration is mirrored in our being. On an individual level vibration is divided into a triune state that reflects the three planes of consciousness. From the center of our being and the universe, a single vibration emanates out in the same manner as a ray of light, which then hits a prism and fragments into three vibrations. These three vibrations are:

1. Life Vibrations (Physical Plane)
2. Mind Vibrations (Mental Plane)
3. Soul Vibrations (Spiritual Plane)

These three vibrations (which in truth are one) govern the universe, so by knowing more of them we can know higher states.

Spiritual vibration is the single emanation out of the eternal center found in all life. Spiritual vibration is connected to the irreducible essence of the universe that we call Tao, Brahman, Allah, God, Universe, Void, and so on. As we ascend higher in the scale of vibration, we begin to know more of this spiritual vibration and God itself.

The majority of beings only attain the scale of life vibrations, as their world is based on the illusion of outward appearance. The mind vibrations are in a state of chaos in those who are not aware of their thoughts. The art of mental alchemy teaches one to be in control of mind-force, which regulates the rate of vibrations in the physical plane. So mind vibrations in the mental plane act as a balancing point between the physical and spiritual planes. Those who are fixated on the physical world are not sovereign over their own mind and are running on a very low vibration, which influences their delusion of separation.

On the other hand those who are sincere in exploring the great work of eternity will find that thoughts and emotions are vibrations. They will realize that becoming sovereign over these illusionary thoughts and emotions embedded in the false ego is imperative. Once they are functioning at this level, they begin to explore mental alchemy and in so doing become conscious creators by following their dharma path. This begins the merging of the mind and soul vibrations, which is the initiation of one entering the spiritual plane. Those who apply mental alchemy while also following their dharma will discover that the light within them is not their own. Through this discovery a miraculous process unfolds, which is the connection between the individual and Divine Will. They then move deeper into the universal center, which is at such a high vibration that it appears as rest, like a rapidly moving wheel that appears stationary. This is a reflection of a being that has dived into the spiritual plane with the note of soul vibrations.

As the notes of the musical scale rise higher and higher, the vibratory motion is increased into an ear-exploding sound that then fades away into silence. Similarly, the science of humility is the highest note or vibration on the eternal strings of divinity. The vibration of those who are moving into the spiritual plane and the cosmic center is at such an infinite rate that it is imperceptible. In this vibration the science of humility is known through the power of silence, which creates the reflection of vibration visualized and felt as divine harmony. Those who move from the mental plane into the spiritual plane know that silence is true power.

We are kept from this eternal peace by many mental energetic blocks, which need to be flushed out before we can truly know ourselves and know the great work of eternity.

COGNITIVE DISSONANCE

Over the ages an epidemic has developed within the mental plane that has suppressed the great work of eternity and the evolution it nurtures. This disease, which has hypnotized a lot of beings— is the prime filth expressed by the false ego, which binds people to illusions. The psychological name for this disease is "cognitive dissonance," and its scientific definition is, "An uncomfortable mental state resulting from conflicting cognitions; usually resolved by changing some of the cognitions."[7]

Cognitive dissonance is what keeps us in a hypnotic sleep that sustains our erroneous belief that the world is outside us. It is the defense mechanism of the ego. The role of cognitive dissonance is to set in concrete on the mental plane all the learned individual belief systems, while keeping the egocentric masses who suffer from this disease ignorant of any new knowledge that may threaten their conditioning. The whole illusion of the ego is that we are what we have learned from birth, and cognitive dissonance ensures none of these beliefs are threatened. The ego is what or who we are not. The ego is everything we have learned from the external world that we attach to our persona. From this point of view we are our thoughts and not the one who is aware of the thoughts.

The main supports of the false ego are: religions, nations, race, and sex. These four pillars of separation offer a perfect example of how cognitive dissonance operates. When the light of knowledge—such as a teaching that we are not our religion or race and so on—is revealed to those who live from the ego, it generates a schizophrenic reaction to the one shining the light. Many avatars throughout eternity have been killed for revealing the truth to those who suffer from cognitive dissonance. In the light of new knowledge, those with a false ego suffer a mental apocalypse, which they project on the one who is liberating them from their mind prison.

Cognitive dissonance is not just bound to the four core pillars of separation; it can be set off in many ways. Most beings have so many blinders or filters functioning within them that it is impossible for them to give new knowledge or information an honest and open hearing. The reflection of pure consciousness in nature is a beautiful flowing river, while the image of cognitive dissonance is a dammed river with water filthy from stagnation. Cognitive dissonance and its parent the ego are what is guiding the human race to destruction and devolution, because those who are caught in these illusions manifest a world full of conflict that reflects their mental state. They contribute to chaos and entropy, instead of order and evolution. The great work of eternity is about opening up to the infinite potential of the cosmos to become the focal point of evolution. It requires applying the art of mental alchemy in the mental plane, following one's dharma, and curing the disease of cognitive dissonance, in order to be receptive to the universal energies and Divine Will.

4

The Evolution of Perception

*W*e can only see reality as it truly is when spiritual consciousness begins to blossom within us. The full comprehension of the spiritual plane can only be complete if we are sincere in our own self-work within the great work of eternity, which is what allows our consciousness to go beyond the physical and mental worlds. The work to be done within the body-mind state of consciousness can be great and fearful, yet it makes possible what has been deemed "the meaning of life." A good majority of beings within this world live on the mental plane of consciousness because escaping the clutches of the mind requires looking into their own psychology and most do not want to do that. But the infinite possibilities and potential of the cosmos open to those who comb out their habitual ways and iron out their latent tendencies (*vasanas* in Sanskrit).

The core objective of one entering the spiritual plane from the mental plane is to merge the individual with the Divine Will.

The union of the individual with the Will of the Divine is the opening of the eternal universe through the finite human vessel. This unification is the true meaning behind the word *yoga,* derived from the root Sanskrit word *yug,* which means "to join" with the Divine or God principle.

Dharma is the expression of this union through the mental virtue of alchemy. The origin of the word *alchemy* is a combination of two words: *Al* is associated with the Arabic word for God, Allah, and also relates to the Hebrew word *El,* which also means God. The word *chem* or *khem* is from the Greek word *kimia* and means to fuse with something. Combining both words we have *al-kimia* or alchemy, which poetically means "to fuse or join with God." Alchemy's esoteric definition reveals the theme of the union between the individual and the Divine hidden deep within the mystery of life. This mystery is comparative with the path of dharma within the universe, but this realization of our own personal virtue is in a sense only there to unravel more profound insights into the nature of our own existence and our position within the universe.

Here lies the axiom at the heart of the spiritual plane of consciousness: when you begin to merge with the Divine Will and allow the universe to flow through you, the science of humility enters your being; it reveals who you truly are and your position within the cosmos. This revelation is usually isolated to the holy sages of eternity. The nature of the unification between the individual and Divine Will is expressed by the wisdom traditions in mystery and parables. In ancient China we hear, "Empty your mind, so the Tao can make use of you." This is reflected in ancient India where we have the primordial phrase, "All is Brahman, and I am That." Found also within the Hermetic teachings from antiquity we have the maxim, "While All is in The All, it is equally true that The All is in All." These three wisdom traditions, just to name a few, are referring to the way in which the totality of the universe works through a human, plus how the Will of the Divine exists in each and every one of us, whether we like it or not.

One parable for this can be found in nature, in the example of the ocean and its numerous waves. Even though we see individual waves rising and crashing, where does a wave start and end? Do the waves part from the ocean? Can they part from the ocean? The obvious answer is "no." Contemplation leads to the question of whether the wave is a wave or the ocean? If we say that the ocean is pure consciousness and the wave is an identity, could our consciousness be separate from the birth of creation and the universe? Again the answer must be "no." But one of the big problems that plagues most beings is identifying with the wave instead of the ocean, which is the foundational understanding of the physical and mental worlds. The greatest leap in the spiritual plane of consciousness is the beginning stages of the identification with the ocean, which leads one to the true evolution.

MOKSHA, A NEW LEVEL OF PERCEPTION

Making this gigantic leap is a very strange undertaking, because the state of consciousness within the spiritual plane is not some sort of holy attitude or way of being overly kind to everybody. Ironically, it is not some type of characteristic you attain that influences others. Rather, you attain a mode of perception, which does not outwardly influence anybody. It does give you the insight to see reality as it truly is. Rather than continuing the attraction of the physical and mental planes to the details of life, to worldly affairs and external appearance, the spiritual plane is an elevated perception of being able to see harmony in all things, even that which to most appears as wars and discord. This is the common trait among all mystics who have existed on Earth and the key to why their love is so unmoving. The spiritual perception of the holy sages throughout eternity is known in Sanskrit as *moksha*.

The three planes of consciousness are in a sense different levels of magnification, with the spiritual plane being the finest form of perception, capable of seeing the universe as it truly is, supporting the ability to understand what the sages have been speaking of when they refer to truth. The teachers of eternity are rarely found and even more rarely understood, because their perspective of the world is an empty state free of judgments and desires. In Richard Wilhelm's translation of the treatise of eternity found in China, known as the *I Ching*, he explains a sage's perception in the following statement.

> Not every man has an obligation to mingle in the affairs of the world. There are some who are developed to such a degree that they are justified in letting the world go its own way and in refusing to enter public life with a view to reforming it. But this does not imply a right to remain idle or to sit back and merely criticize. Such withdrawal is justified only when we strive to realize in ourselves the higher aims of mankind. For although the sage remains distant from the turmoil of daily life, he creates incomparable human values for the future.[1]

The common erroneous preconception of teachers of eternity is that they are somewhat selfish because they do not partake in the mundane affairs of the world. But, is it more selfish to have an agenda for the world and try to impose it on others or being constantly in introspection and partaking in the great work of eternity? The fact of the matter is that those who only know of the physical and mental planes are still hypnotized by their egos and bound by their identity; those in this psychosis can never help the world because their idea of a peaceful world is attuned to their own personal comforts and conveniences. Thus they have an agenda for everybody else.

Those suffering from this delusion want to uproot tyranny and oppose a system that is fundamentally flawed, but they only aggravate the problem. Dwelling within the body-mind state of consciousness, they are trying to heal a chaotic world with a chaotic mind. Those who believe they are only the identity or ego believe in separation, which is the seed of chaos. A chaotic universe cannot be healed through the eyes of separation. The fundamental flaw does not exist in the environment—composed of a tyrannical group, government, or system, on the contrary—the flaw exists in each and every one of us. Teacher of eternity Sri Nisargadatta Maharaj exemplified this when he said, "First realise that your world is but a reflection of yourself and stop finding fault with the reflection."[2]

THE VISION OF CHAOS

A teacher of eternity does not see chaos, but she knows why others do, so she knows why it exists. The masses believe that if the chaos of the world—such as political, social, or religious—can be rectified, then a natural order will follow that will lead us to our next evolutionary step. Nothing could be further from the truth.

Evolution does not depend on outward progress and the order of a society; it is dependent upon the growth of the individual. The illusion of evolution is that it is associated with material progress in the external world. As we have stated earlier, evolution is the growth of consciousness in the individual. However, this is very vague in its meaning and only half the picture. What is meant by growth? Are we speaking about knowledge or perception? Evolution does not begin in the knowledge we gain from the world within or without; it is discovered in the way we view ourselves and the universe around us. The insight into the spiritual plane of consciousness is that evolution is the awareness that is at the very ground of our being. This awareness is the authentic definition of evolution or growth in consciousness, which is known in the great work of eternity as the evolution of perception.

The evolution of perception is born in one who is no longer attracted to the separate little fragments of reality and begins seeing the universe—from an electron to the totality of the cosmos—as an interdependent whole functioning in a rhythm almost musical in nature, beyond intellectual reasoning. The core of the spiritual plane is the awareness that the universe is not something separate from you or outside of you, but instead is one living breathing conscious organism and you are an integral part of that. The true evolution of perception gives you the eyes of the universe to see that all of the war and discord we have on one level is actually harmony on a higher level; all of this chaos in a sense is necessary as it makes up the rhythm of the eternal harmony.

The holy sages of eternity do not see chaos because their consciousness is rooted in the center of their being, which is the center of the universe. It is almost like they see the world from a vantage point above. Such teachers have always expounded that suffering does not exist, because they see reality in its true complete state. This enlightened state of consciousness is hard for individuals bound by beliefs to understand. This explains why the masses judge an enlightened master as selfish and why many masters have been sacrificed: they can see reality while the masses are still slaves to their own minds. Inner slavery is the result of the obstinate refusal to discard the beliefs we have been indoctrinated with, which keeps the mental plane in a state of movement and never at rest, thus we have chaos reflected into the projection of the physical plane. The sage, on the other hand, has a clear mental state, one that reflects space and allows the cosmic dharma to flow through and manifest as order on Earth. Here the universal polarities of chaos and order are seen in a different light, as the natural ebb and flow of consciousness.

ORDO AB CHAO

The slogan "order out of chaos" is the English translation of the Latin proverb *ordo ab chao*. The consensus belief is that this phrase refers to a situation in which a group of people, such as a government, religion, or sect, create circumstances causing a society to become unsteady, which inevitably moves into chaos, then the very same people who created the situation offer their own order as a solution. On a physical and mental level this version makes complete sense, but it is only a superficial comprehension.

The occult knowledge that lies at the heart of "order out of chaos" is the evolution of perception. Chaos and order in their esoteric essence are the two different modes of awareness within the cosmos. The chaotic mode is caught in the detail of life and the order sees The All in All. So "order out of chaos" really means the individual transformation of consciousness to perceive the harmony of the universe rather than being caught in the web of life that the conditioned ego believes to be chaotic. Like an eagle soaring high above worldly affairs, one can see that all things are in their right place.

A common theme of order out of chaos and the evolution of perception can be seen in ancient symbolism. The image in figure 4.1 is the seal of the 33rd degree (the highest degree possible for initiates) of Scottish Rite Freemasonry. Within this seal we find the phrase *ordo ab chao* and we see a double-headed eagle. The double-headed eagle refers to one who has knowledge of the two primal energies of the cosmos that create the conscious universe. As mentioned earlier, these primal energies can be understood as yang/Heaven/masculine/creative/positive and yin/Earth/feminine/receptive/negative. Having digested this knowledge, we attain the eagle's eyes of perception, or in other words, the ability to see order out of chaos; hence we discover the evolution of perception.

Figure 4.1. Seal of Scottish Rite Freemasonry, 33rd degree
By Daniel A. Stewart

There are certain common misconceptions about this symbol pertaining to the imagery of the crown and the number 33. They are erroneously associated with the 33rd degree of Scottish Rite of Freemasonry, which is deemed to be an elitist group. Another popular belief is that both refer to the life of Jesus. All of these are true on a superficial level. The story of Jesus could be perceived in the allegorical view that it took thirty-three years or steps of his life to reach enlightenment, which is associated with the crown. But there is a deeper meaning. First of all we need to look at the origins of Christianity. Christianity at its core is relatively newly hatched from two of the oldest religions on the planet, Hinduism and Buddhism. A lot of its spiritual knowledge was also taken from the Gnostic adepts of that era.

The Christian religion is based on the life and teachings of Jesus, but what did Jesus know and where did he gain his wisdom? The answer to this is found in the eighteen years of Jesus's life that the masses are told not to inquire into. In those lost years Jesus embarked on a spiritual journey to the Orient, most notably India, where he learned from many masters about Hinduism and the way of Gautama the Buddha. Both Hinduism and Buddhism speak of the sage from the West known as "Saint Issa." Isa is the Arabic name for Jesus in Islam and Issa is the Sanskrit name for Jesus. Numerous manuscripts found in India and Tibet mention the life of St. Issa in India, where he gained his eternal wisdom. When Jesus came back to the Middle East, he brought with him the wisdom of the East and the esoteric systems of knowledge, which gave birth to Christianity. The influence of both Eastern religions can be found most notably within the *Gospel of Thomas* and the *Nag Hammadi* texts.

Both the crown and 33 are occult properties of Hinduism

that are very significant. The Hindu methodology of attaining enlightenment has a template for understanding how the body is related to the spiritual plane of consciousness: the knowledge that there are seven energetic centers within the human body, called *chakras* in Sanskrit. These seven chakras are a reflection of the seven chakras of the Earth, our solar system, Milky Way galaxy, and the universe. In the human body the seven chakras are always depicted as rising up the spinal column. The seventh chakra is located at the top of the skull and is called the "crown chakra"; it is the connection between the eternal and the manifest, which is the merging into enlightenment. The first chakra, called the "root chakra," is located at the base of the spine. In Hinduism, Buddhism, and other ancient traditions, there is the knowledge that a dormant energy of the universe lies at the base of the spine until it is wakened. This is commonly known as the *kundalini,* the serpent energy. It is symbolized by the Caduceus of Hermes with two snakes rising up a shaft, as is seen in figure 4.2.

Figure 4.2. Caduceus of Hermes

The two snakes are a reflection of the double-headed eagle as well as of the ida and pingala, the mystical channels entwined along the spine. The kundalini, like the double-headed eagle, has to travel to a place of seeing the world from above to gain the vision of the universe in its truth. In the kundalini's case, it has to travel from the root chakra all the way to the crown chakra. This journey holds the secret of 33, which connects Hinduism, Buddhism, Christianity, and the allegory behind the thirty-three years of Jesus. For kundalini to travel to the crown chakra, the source of immutable light, it needs to traverse the thirty-three vertebrae of the spine. The path to the crown is not something one should aspire to in the physical world of hierarchy; it is in truth the attainment of the holy sages known as the evolution of perception. So the wisdom behind the crown and thirty-three is the essence of what they represent: the capacity of an enlightened master to see order out of chaos and thus further evolution through their own being.

When we gain insight into the structure of the three planes of consciousness, we find each one overlapping the other. For instance, the crown and 33 refer to the evolution of perception, yet we could not gain that insight without exploring the esoteric anatomy of the body as consciousness. In doing so we see that the spiritual plane exists within the physical plane, so we again have evidence that the physical world is consciousness. Though this is true, only those who dwell on the spiritual plane know it; instead of looking at the illusion of separation, they see the universe as a single organism.

The evolution of perception is the authentic evolution because it is the ultimate growth of the individual. Such evolution is an isolated event and is hard to translate to those still affected by the chaotic mind of the ego. The spiritual plane of consciousness is a higher level of magnification than the body-mind state, but, that being so, a question presents itself. If the three planes that build the fabric of reality—physical, mental, and spiritual—are all aspects of our consciousness, which level of magnification is the truth? This is an interesting question, because if all is consciousness, could one level be more truthful than the other? We could say that those who dwell within the physical and mental planes or body-mind state are under the spell of the deluded mind and do not know their true self nor their place within the universe. At the same time, those on the spiritual plane know who they truly are and can see reality as it truly is through the evolution of perception. But even though those in one state know the truth of evolution and those in the other are still slaves to the ego, does this make one more truthful than the other?

The fact is they are all the truth in the sense that all levels have to be there to make up what we call existence. Without the one focusing on the illusion of daily struggles and the detail of life, we could not have the one who sees harmony from a higher perspective. One cannot exist without the other. To perceive harmony we need the intrinsic parts that make up the formation of what we see. So all levels need to exist to have reality itself. When we mention truth, we are not saying one level is better than another, but rather pointing to the correct way to see the totality of existence through our focal point of consciousness.

The fundamental truth does not reside in the levels of consciousness, but in the awareness itself. It depends on the perceiver. The individual who sees the world as it is has had an overwhelming transformation. The way in which the universe moves in its flow and patterned harmony is within our consciousness as well.

We either know this or we don't. It is the way we see the world that holds us to what "is" and "isn't." There are those who perpetually get caught in the details of life and those who see the universe as it truly is. Consciousness is not only the foundation of the universe, but it is the whole universe. As we have explored the holy sage's perception is a mirror reflection of how the universe is, which is called the evolution of perception.

5

The Way of the Warrior and Path of the Sage

❧❧

A human has two primary states of awareness or modes of being. As we have mentioned there are those who are drawn into the daily dramas of life and those who have an elevated perspective, capable of seeing a fractal harmony within all life. These two states of awareness run parallel with the conscious state of the false ego and the true self, respectively. The ego perceives the fine details of reality. Like a microscope the ego focuses on the very tiny matters of life, then mistakenly builds its psychology around these insignificant situations. On the other hand the true self is the state of consciousness so pure that it constantly sees that life is pattern; in this state the unfolding universe can be visualized. This state of awareness is a mind of no deliberation, a mind that does not attach itself to any circumstance or thought—past, present, or future. The true self dwells within the spiritual plane and knows the soul vibrations, hence the evolution of perception. We associate this state of consciousness with a teacher of eternity or a sage, and the state of consciousness of the ego caught in the details with the masses or the profane. Both primary states of awareness are built into the universal structure. These two viewpoints have been an area of confusion throughout the ages. Yet both are necessary and together form a cosmic law.

The teacher and student relationship is found in all levels of life, whether as parent and child, teacher and student, or— the most mysterious of all—master and disciple. In the immutable relationship between master and disciple, the disciple is still deluded by the mind, whereas the master knows the totality of our being. These two modes are represented in ancient scriptures and mystical stories as "the warrior" and "the sage." Many examples of a sage teaching a warrior are found in the Vedantic treatises of India, most notably the *Bhagavad Gita* and *Ribhu Gita* (Song of Ribhu). The *Bhagavad Gita* tells the story of Arjuna the warrior and Krishna the sage, while the *Ribhu Gita* refers to Nidagha the warrior and Ribhu the sage. In both classics the warrior is suffering from his own mind and plight within this world. As he begins to question his mind, the guidance of the sage appears. In both scriptures the whole process is to lift the warrior's mode of perception out of the details of life into the vision of the Divine. In the *Bhagavad Gita* Krishna attempts to move Arjuna's awareness out of the daily mundane struggles of life into the vision of Brahman, which is to see the infinite in all things. Verses 31, 32, and 33 of chapter 13 of the *Bhagavad Gita* state:

> *When a sensible man ceases to see different*
> *identities due to different material bodies and*

he sees how beings are expanded everywhere,
he attains to the Brahman conception.

Those with the vision of eternity can see
that the imperishable soul is transcendental,
eternal, and beyond the modes of nature.
Despite contact with the material body, O
Arjuna, the soul neither does anything nor is
entangled.

The sky, due to its subtle nature, does not mix
with anything, although it is all-pervading.
Similarly, the soul situated in Brahman vision
does not mix with the body, though situated in
that body.[1]

This is only one of many ways to interpret these scriptures, but this way of understanding the relationship between the warrior and sage is imperative to the practice of the science of humility. These two modes of being correspond to the flow of chaos (warrior) and order (sage) within consciousness. One of the biggest problems to plague this planet throughout time has been the fostering of the warrior's consciousness and the continual suppression of the sage's consciousness. It comes back to the individual, so there is no one to blame for this other than ourselves. Our obstinate refusal to look within ourselves to find the true problems in our world has allowed us to further justify our own habitual ways that are slowly killing the human species. For us to ward off this fate, we need to understand where our awareness is rooted. To do this we need to explore the characteristics of a warrior and a sage.

THE WARRIOR

The warrior is an ephemeral state of awareness that gets swept up in trying to change the world. To achieve this implied change, warriors attempt to impose their will on others. In the belief they are striving for world peace, they cause more trauma. The warrior does not know that fighting for a solution only increases a problem. Why do we fight? Here "fight," means to have conflict or oppose some situation either within or without.

One of the major dilemmas of the human psyche is having the notion that something is either good or bad. When an individual judges if something is good or bad, it comes back to the false psychological state known as the ego: humans judge if something is good or bad according to their own conditioning from birth. Not being conscious of this, warriors seek to change the world according to their likes and dislikes. So a warrior does not truly want to bring peace to the world because he is in fact conspiring against it. The majority of beings on Earth have a warrior's consciousness, which is evident in the chaos of the physical and mental worlds. Those who believe that what is right for them is the way for everybody else are not truly concerned about another being's authentic way of life.

A warrior harbors an artificial internal conspiracy, that of believing that we are our thoughts and our accumulated conditioning. Buying into the grand delusion of conditioning fragments reality into chaos and separation. The warrior knows the chattering within the mind but is ignorant of the one who hears the thoughts. As warriors are only conscious of the physical and mental planes, they ignorantly perpetuate their beliefs of separation. These beliefs usually fall into the categories of political, religious, social, and so on.

If you are taking upon yourself the responsibility to change the world, on whose authority are you doing this? Is this through your dharma, which inspires others, or a belief system that you want to uphold? Warriors who try to push their personal agenda upon others through any means necessary get caught up in hatred and violence toward those who oppose that agenda. The question we need to ask is whether the world needs to change and according to whose plans?

As the warrior is projecting all of her inner falsified qualities on to the world, surely the salvation that needs to take place is within the individual. Those who are stuck in the awareness of a warrior, and are drawn into worldly affairs with an illusion of changing the status quo to their liking, will only contribute to decay on all levels of life, leading to the annihilation of the race. Real evolution has nothing to do with changing finite matters; it is only found by stepping out of worldly affairs with a determination to change the individual who sees the world.

THE SAGE

The great work of eternity is about refining the consciousness to a single point. This refined consciousness allows the individual to bring the eternal virtue of the science of humility into the manifest world. The single-pointed consciousness we are speaking of is not snagged by any thought, emotion, or external circumstance, because the awareness is rooted in the universal perspective. The one who knows the science of humility knows that to try to control any aspect of the universe is futile.

A sage is someone who is sincere in the search for the eternal within. Those with the evolved consciousness of a sage do not put off enlightenment for their next life as they know truth is only here and now. Nothing distracts their focus on how to truly see themselves and the totality of the cosmos. This is a major difference between a warrior and a sage: a warrior remains distracted by external events while a sage sees distractions as mental projections of the ego, and turns inward to see the true source of the problem. By turning within the sage realizes that the result of perceiving the world through the eyes of individual conditioning is that all judgments and desires are not based in the foundation of one's being. A sage then seeks to eradicate latent tendencies and habitual ways of thinking from his consciousness. For warriors this is a scary undertaking, because the majority of beings on this planet will do anything to distract themselves from facing their own psyche. Sages do not see this as scary but as imperative to evolution and salvation. As they begin to move away from all of the external noise, more space begins to enter their being, which gives them the crystal clear clarity of how to see through the universal eye.

DEFINING THE DIFFERENCE

The subjective consciousness of the warrior is caught in the details while the objective consciousness of the sage sees correctly. In all esoteric work the whole purpose of any system is to take us from a subjective worldview to an objective reality. The more we refine our consciousness, the more we begin to access this objective reality.

Upon self-reflection the sage sees that what he wanted for the world and himself was attuned to his egocentric conditioning. So the process of ridding himself of his own inner conspiracy doesn't end until the very last remnant of illusion is combed out.

This process is what moves the sage from being concerned with worldly affairs. A sage knows fundamentally that to truly change the world, we need to change where the world comes from. And where it comes from is the individual's perception of it. This is a bitter pill to swallow for some, because this means that force actually never truly changes anything. At best it may provide a momentary Band-Aid for a situation.

Force and humility are the two virtues that distinguish a warrior from a sage. Warriors see external events and seek to change them to suit their conditioning, yet this is a process of forcing their own version of reality upon others. In most cases this appears as a revolution. It doesn't matter whether it is the overthrowing of a particular political party, religious group, or social system; they are all only temporary solutions from the same ground of the ego. Warriors do not see that they have their own agenda to perpetuate. What is most astonishing is that the inner and outer actions of the warrior actually imply that the universal design of creation is faulty and that God made a mistake. A warrior would not question the structure of his own abode, so how could he ignorantly question the structural design of consciousness? The illusion of separation continues to distort the universe through this ignorant mode of awareness until the vanity of the warrior is exposed through a fight that cannot and will not be won.

The sage, on the other hand, knows that no matter how hard we try, we will never defeat the universe and its unfoldment. The sage knows that life is pattern and each fragment of the universe is connected to every other part; nothing can escape this cosmic web. The sage sees no reason to fight because she is attuned to the universal harmony from her elevation of consciousness. Sages know it is absurd to question the design of the universe, so instead seek to find how they are part of the universe. Through their inner exploration, sages discover that the universe is in constant change and that this universal process is unfolding within them as well. So the grand choice becomes apparently clear: we can either fight the universal stream, or we can swim with it. We can force ourselves upon the universe, or become humble students of it.

The gulf of understanding between a warrior and a sage has been with humanity since ancient times. The teacher of eternity known as Chuang-tzu once described an imaginary dialogue between two of the great masters of antiquity, Confucius and Lao-tzu. It is believed that Confucius was a disciple of Lao-tzu. In this dialogue you will see a conversation between a warrior and a sage beautifully depicted.

"Tell me," said Lao-tzu, "in what consist charity and duty to one's neighbour?"

"They consist," answered Confucius, "in a capacity for rejoicing in all things; in universal love, without the element of self. These are the characteristics of charity and duty to one's neighbour."

"What stuff!" cried Lao-tzu. "Does not universal love contradict itself? Is not your elimination of self a positive manifestation of self? Sir, if you would cause the empire not to lose its source of nourishment—there is the universe, its regularity is unceasing; there are the sun and moon, their brightness is unceasing; there are the stars, their groupings never change; there are the birds and beasts, they flock together without varying; there are the trees and shrubs, they grow upward without exception. Be like these: follow Tao, and you will be perfect. Why then these vain struggles after charity and duty to one's

Figure 5.1. Confucius and Lao-tzu in dialogue
By Jiwon Kim (Lathandar)

neighbour, as though beating a drum in search of a fugitive. Alas! Sir, you have brought much confusion into the mind of man."[2]

The unfoldment of the universe is always teaching us that no matter how hard we try, things are just as they are supposed to be. On another level they are paradoxically viewed as problems to be overcome. These two ways of perception are built into the fabric of the universe, with both a warrior and a sage playing their role in the grand unfoldment of the cosmos. While warriors see separate parts and seek to change them, the sage sees the totality of the universe. The sage does not fight anything either within or without, because distinctions do not exist for a sage. The sage begins to act and move as the universe does, and the evolution of perception brings the realization that the focus of attention that the warrior possesses is only a part of the universal makeup.

The sage's revelation is the understanding that even if warriors aspire to go beyond the mind and reach enlightenment, they will always fall short. Even though the goal is higher, trying to reach it by fighting will not be successful. Ultimately the sage reveals the wisdom of the universe: that no matter how hard you try, you cannot hold on to yourself. This is what is referred to by terms such as samadhi, satori, and enlightenment. As a reflection of the universe a sage will change with it. The process of the universe is not something that takes gigantic leaps; it moves in very small stages. So the movement of perception from that of a warrior to that of a sage is a constant flow of conscious energy. Like a mountain stream the universal stream moves in a fluid motion without being attached to what is perceived as external reality; in not being caught anywhere, it moves toward the larger body of water.

6
Primal Rhythm

❧

*T*he natural flow or stream of consciousness is in a constant process of expansion and contraction. Within an individual's awareness this process of expansion and contraction takes place through the flux of chaos and order. This is how the false ego gets swept up in daily affairs, while the true self perceives the eternal harmony in all life. The warrior and a sage are the modes of being that exhibit these two states of awareness. The warrior is deluded by the physical and mental planes, while the sage is rooted in the spiritual plane.

From the elevated state of a sage, separation does not exist, not even between the different ways a warrior and a sage perceive the world. The evolution of perception reveals that enlightenment is not a fixed end or goal, but instead is a way of flowing with the universal stream. A sage is in the flow of the cosmos and is not attached to any belief about himself either within or without. His mind is as empty as the space that holds the universe together.

The space of the universe and the solid worlds within it are a reflection of the three planes of consciousness within a sentient life-form. The manifest world arises from the movement of attraction and repulsion within the unmanifest space of the universe. The microcosm works in the same fashion, where we discover the attraction and repulsion of the physical and mental plane functioning within the spiritual plane. Yet we cannot have the unmanifest without the manifest; likewise we cannot have the spiritual plane without the physical and mental worlds.

This brings us face to face with a subtle paradox: even though we can never hold on to ourselves consciously, the vibratory world of the physical and mental worlds holds us within a physical body. We can never hold on to our identity, but we still find ourselves defined as an identity in the manifest world. As an ancient Zen proverb states:

> *Before enlightenment*
> *chopping wood*
> *carrying water.*
> *After enlightenment*
> *chopping wood*
> *carrying water.*[1]

The mysterious nature of the universal stream of consciousness is such that we can either let go of our conditioned identity and flow with the universe, or we can continue to cling to the riverbank of fear, but no matter how hard we try to hold on, we will have to let go one day. Nothing we have conditioned ourselves with can be held on to, because we are not outside of the universal stream. The more we swim against it, the more we will struggle. So what or who we believe we are cannot be maintained.

A paradox exists here because on one hand we cannot completely let go of our physical body, yet on the other hand our identity cannot be held on to. This is the mystery behind moksha, samadhi, satori, enlightenment, and so on. The paradox exists because of how the universe acts, moves, and is. The universe is in constant movement and consciousness is the mirror reflection of that; this state of change is something that also pertains to the teachers of eternity. The constant change that a sage begins to perceive is governed by the harmony found on all planes of consciousness. Built into the fabric of reality itself, this is known to the masters as the "law of change."

THE LAW OF CHANGE

Teachings about the law of change can be seen as a common thread within all wisdom traditions. The law of change is actually the "law of Tao" or "law of evolution." All these refer to the universal stream of all life. The amazing thing about the changing world is how the expansion and contraction of consciousness builds the idea of change. The two modes of being exemplify this: a warrior's attention gets caught in individual transitory things, while a sage perceives the harmony within all things. From the elevated view of a sage, even chaos is in harmony. This harmony is itself immutable and governed by an eternal law. The eternal law is the way the Tao, or Brahman, or God, or Allah, moves to create harmony on all planes. The law of changes is the very law that governs the eternal harmony.

The sage, with his consciousness fixed in its correct position, can see this law at work in all change, almost like watching the Divine at play. We could say the sage is perceiving the breath of the Absolute through the law that constitutes change. The connection between the individual and Divine Will allows the awareness of the law underlying change through the evolution of perception. One attuned to higher levels of perception will know the law esoterically through its flowing motion.

Sometimes there are objections to the use of the term *law* to refer to this unceasing change. Yet think of it this way: Can you stop the cyclic motion of day and night or the seasons? The answer obviously is "No." The majority of humans have a fear of being governed by any external source, yet no one can escape this law, even if we don't believe so. The idea that we are not subject to the law is the same as thinking we are separate from the universe.

Throughout time, spiritually proud ignoramuses have thought of this law as something to be overcome. This is nothing more than a trick of the ego, because knowing the true self means knowing that this law of change is an aspect of consciousness. The erroneous belief about the need to transcend it arises from the intellectual understanding that within the center of each of us is a non-dual space governed by no external law. This is true, yet those who truly know the center know that eternity is comprehended through the manifest world, which is bound by the law of change.

If you were to know the Eternal Self and only that, then you would not be able to read these words, as you would disappear into the unmanifest. On the other hand, if you are reading these words, then you know that the ego is an aspect of consciousness, which holds the key to the law of change and the evolution of perception. This is the paradox we have spoken of, because in order to know the science of humility, you need to know all aspects of your being, which includes the vibratory awareness of the warrior within the physical and mental planes of consciousness.

How we are part of the law of change is a mystery that leads to enlightenment. If we try to understand this process of change within the universe intellectually, then we will be thwarted by egotistical snags of the mind. But if we are truly seeking to know, then we will discover that eternity is revealed by more abstract knowledge. The abstract is where all profound insights reveal themselves. The various wisdom traditions explain the principle of the universe in flowery abstract language, because to understand our being we need to go beyond the mind.

THE BREATH OF BRAHMA

Hinduism refers to the breath of Brahma. Brahma is depicted as the source of life at the primordial center of the universe. The breath of Brahma is the expansion and contraction of consciousness. It refers to the constant in and out action between focusing on the details of life and seeing reality from above. This in and out motion of the breath is comparable to the principle of "involution," or the subjective view of the world, and "evolution," or objective view of the world, found most notably within Hermeticism and other occult traditions. These parallel the different modes of perception of a warrior and a sage. The ebb and flow of these two states creates the idea of change.

In certain wisdom traditions we also find knowledge of the "law of octaves," in which the two modes of involution and evolution are characterized in relation to the musical scale. In the eternal treatise known as *The Reality of Being: The Fourth Way of Gurdjieff,* written by the eternal teacher Jeanne de Salzmann, she explains the teachings of the Armenian mystic George Ivanovich Gurdjieff and how the law of octaves can either deepen our perception of higher states of vibration or how it can distract us from our own source of being.

> *The Law of Octaves (the Law of Seven)*. All matter in the universe consists of vibrations descending toward manifestation of form ("involution"), or ascending in a return to the formless source ("evolution"). Their development is not continuous but characterized by periodic accelerations and retardations at definite intervals. The laws governing this process are embodied in an ancient formula that divides the period in which a vibration doubles into eight unequal steps corresponding to the rate of increase in the vibrations. This period is called an "octave," that is to say, "composed of eight." This formula lies at the basis of the Biblical myth of the creation of the world, and our division of time into workdays and Sundays. Applied to music, the formula is expressed in the musical scale *do-re-mi-fa-sol-la-si-do*, with semitones missing at the intervals *mi-fa* and *si-do*. The inner movement toward consciousness requires a "conscious shock" at these two intervals in order to proceed to a higher level, that is, a new octave.[2]

Involution means "to be involved" or, in other words, to be lost in worldly affairs, while evolution means "a way out of this involvement," where one is perched upon a plateau with an elevated view. The alternation between the two states is like breath moving in and out. A sage knows this and moves in correspondence to the ebb and flow of the cosmos, but they are more rooted in the elevated state. The involution and evolution of the universe is what maintains the law of change. The breath illustrates this most poignantly, because holding on to either the in-breath or out-breath, without letting the breath function naturally, inevitably brings death. Likewise is the alternation of perception between that of a warrior and a sage. We could not have consciousness without these changing states, as we cannot have order without chaos.

The knowledge of the breath of Brahma and involution and evolution exists to show us that no matter how hard we try, we cannot stop change. The insight possessed by a sage is that no matter what you do to hold on to yourself, you cannot. The mystery is that when you understand the law of change, then you know more about the enlightenment of the changeless. In ancient China the eternal treatise known as the *I Ching* (or *Book of Changes* in English) was laid out to explore the abstract center, through the changing world of the manifest. The *I Ching* is the result of the intuitive works of four holy sages: Fu His, King Wen, the Duke of Chou, and Confucius. The *Book of Changes* came about through the contemplations of these holy sages on the Tao. As we have said the Tao is the equivalent to Brahman, All, God, Allah, and so on; all refer to the irreducible essence of the universe. The *I Ching* is an exploration of the course of "things" in correspondence to the principle of the one and the many, how the individual and the cosmos are related and how both are in constant change. Standing by a river, Confucius once said, "Everything flows on and on like this river, without pause, day and night."[3]

Change is not something that can be stopped, as it is an aspect of consciousness. But which part of consciousness does change belong to? Change belongs to the physical and mental planes of consciousness, as they are what shape and mold the manifest world. The mental force that creates the physical world is what builds the idea of change. The *I Ching* is composed of sixty-four hexagrams, made up of six lines that are either broken or unbro-

Figure 6.1 The first hexagram of the I *Ching:*
Ch'ien (The Creative)

Figure 6.2. The second hexagram of the I *Ching:*
K'un (The Receptive)

ken, all possible combinations. The first two hexagrams describe the mental transformations of physical matter. The first hexagram is *Ch'ien* (The Creative) (see figure 6.1); the six unbroken lines stand for Heaven/active/positive/masculine. In the second hexagram *K'un* (The Receptive) (see figure 6.2) the six broken lines stand for Earth/passive/negative/feminine.

The Creative and the Receptive give birth to spirit and matter. The mental plane is the masculine force of the cosmos and the physical plane is the feminine receptivity of the cosmos. Most wisdom traditions erroneously associate God with being a male, because the masculine energy is what creates, yet nothing could be created without the receptive feminine energy. We can never have one without the other, hence God is both masculine and feminine, or we could say "androgynous." Or we could put it this way: We could not have the physical without the mental plane and vice versa. This also corresponds to the "law of three" found in various wisdom traditions, where positive and negative forces arise out of a neutral aspect, and both need to be reconciled back within the neutral to gain wisdom. The law of three is nothing more than the three planes of consciousness, where we find the relationship of positive/mental/masculine and negative/physical/feminine, both of which are aspects of the non-dual neutral/spiritual/androgynous.

Change then exists in the distinction between the two, which builds the concept of duality. The warrior sees only duality instead of the real world. The ability to see the law and its harmony within all life only arises when we unify the masculine and feminine or physical and mental. The unification of the masculine and feminine allows us to be holy or, we could say, "to be whole," which is the complete state that has a direct link to the Absolute. Likewise when we comprehend the alignment of the physical and mental planes, we then dwell on the spiritual plane, thus having a connection to the Divine. In discovering this we come back to the evolution of perception: the sage sees the harmony, the law in all things, and contemplates "The All in the All" in what is perceived as change. The consciousness of the sage is fixed on the eternal flow of the universe and the exploration of what is behind the changing manifestation. In Hermetic philosophy there is the search for "The All" in the changing world. One of the eternal treatises, the *Kybalion,* states, "Under, and back of, the Universe of Time, Space and Change, is ever to be found The Substantial Reality—the Fundamental Truth."[4]

The fundamental truth is what lies behind the changing world. Those who contemplate this discover that in the manifest world life lacks an enduring quality. All forms of life go through a process of birth, growth, decay, and death. Like the breath, everything rises and falls, expands and contracts, with inflow and outflow, birth and death, and so on. Nothing escapes this process, except for one thing: change. The permanence of change is the only enduring quality of the physical and mental planes. The holy sages of antiquity always contemplated change because it is eternal. This is the connection between the manifest world and that of the unmanifest: change is an expression of eternity that we can become conscious of. The sages who have explored change have found that the entire process of birth, growth, decay, and death is confined to an operation of "rhythm," which reverberates from the spiritual into the physical plane. The expansion and contraction of consciousness is tuned to this rhythm. This rhythm is what gives music its sound, light its brightness, and dance its flamboyant movement. The permanence of change as a rhythm, as the ebb and flow of the universal stream, is expressed by the fifth universal law of Hermes Trismegistus.

V. The Principle of Rhythm

Everything flows, out and in; everything has its tides; all things rise and fall; the pendulum-swing manifests in everything; the measure of the swing to the right is the measure of the swing to the left; rhythm compensates.[5]

The evolution of perception is about hearing and visualizing this rhythm playing out. The ancient wisdom traditions often referred to hearing the "song of God." Observing this song unfold, the ancient sages of the Orient devised a system of yugas to map the rhythm of the universe. A complex doctrine of four world ages, the yugas map the cycles of change. Two systems of yugas have been derived, both based on the concept of *kalpa,* a Sanskrit word that means an "eon" in Hindu and Buddhist cosmology. A kalpa equals 4.32 billion years as it is described in the ancient texts of the *Puranas,* especially the *Vishnu Purana* and *Bhagavata Purana.* The 4.32 billion years is regarded as a day of Brahma, which is the equivalent to one kalpa. In the long count system, one kalpa is made up of one thousand *maha-yugas.* The duration of a maha-yuga is built on four yugas.

Satya (ideal or truthful) *Yuga* (1,728,000 years)
Treta (virtue declined by a quarter) *Yuga* (1,296,000 years)
Dvapara (virtue reduced by half) *Yuga* (864,000 years)
Kali (virtue reduced to a quarter) *Yuga* (432,000 years)

The long count system of the maha-yugas is so vast that it is impossible to assume which yuga we are now currently in. For this very reason a smaller and more precise system of the yugas has been constructed on the understanding of a universal rhythm of time found in relation to human history and the position of our sun around its dual. In this system the sun and its dual make one complete orbit around each other every 24,000 years. The smaller system is based on the science of how the cosmos is in relation to the rhythm and consciousness both individually and collectively, which is much like the ancient divination art of astrology. In this form of the yugas the ages not only map the external world, but also reveal that the external world is a reflection of the internal world. So the yugas in this form are associated with states of consciousness that define the dharma of that particular age. The smaller count is set out in four ages separated into two, resulting in eight ages that mirror each other. In the small count we have,

Satya Yuga 9,600 years (Spiritual Age)
Treta Yuga 7,200 years (Mental Age)
Dvapara Yuga 4,800 years (Energy Age)
Kali Yuga 2,400 years (Material Age)

The science of the yugas can be proven by historical markers, but this is not their deeper significance. Their cycle is itself in a rhythm, which attempts to describe change. One full cycle of 24,000 years goes through 12,000 years of descent and then another 12,000 years of ascension. This again corresponds with the breath and the movement of rhythm. The yugas exemplify the rhythm of the changing universe both within the individual and the macrocosm. And they present the fact that no matter what age one is in, there is no end nor beginning, as the cycle continues to ebb and flow. This could only be visualized from an elevated state. A sage who dwells on the spiritual plane can see that all change is the result of this rhythm, which moves in and out like a breath.

7
Patterned Vibration

※

*A*s the cosmic breath continues to flow in and out, all things rise and fall; the cycle remains a constant in this eternal process. The rhythm of change is the one thing that nothing escapes, not even a sage, yet this rhythm only pertains to the physical and mental planes. All manifest things that come into existence attain a physical form with a mental intelligence within it. Everything from the mineral, plant, animal, and human kingdoms has an intelligence that is collectively part of consciousness. As we mentioned the physical is controlled by the mental vibrations; thus the manifest world is itself vibration. Vibration, like rhythm, is a constant. It is caused by the friction of spirit and matter, the creative and the receptive, or we could say, the spiritual and mental/physical planes.

The eternal movement of change causes vibration to manifest the song of the universe. As the physical world is made up of a combination of vibration and rhythm, it has its own sounding tones that are not perceptible to the human ear. Teacher of eternity Samael Aun Weor once stated:

Any motion is coessential to sound. Wherever motion exists, sound too exists. The human ear is only capable of perceiving a limited number of sound vibrations. Nonetheless, above and below the sound vibrations that the human ear can perceive, there exist multiple sound waves that the human ear is not capable of perceiving (i.e., the fish of the sea produce their own peculiar sounds). The ants communicate among themselves by means of sounds that are inaudible to our range of physical perception. Sounding waves, acting upon water produce the motion of elevation and the pressure of the waters. Sounding waves, acting upon the air, produce concentric movements. The atoms spinning around their nuclear centers produce certain sounds that are imperceptible to humans. Fire, air, water and earth have their own particular sounding notes.[1]

Sound crystallizes the physical world, but sound can be heard on many different levels. On one level we have the sound of music, yet on another level we have the thought vibrations of the mental plane, which create the physical world. One is heard and the other we know exists because we think and feel. Sound is a combination of vibration and rhythm that can harmonize life or destroy it. All forms of sound can lift us higher or bring us down. We only have to look at language orally transmitted to see that the vibration of speech can be in a beautiful rhythm or form words that can be harmful to another being. Thoughts also can do this, especially if we are not conscious of our internal landscape. We can be taken down to the depths, described in Buddhism as the "hells." If we dwell only on the physical and mental planes, then the sound emanating from our consciousness will be attuned to the false ego, which creates a disharmonic state. On the other hand, those who are in the heart of the spiritual plane will be living their dharma in connection with the Divine, harmoniously helping others to move out of the illusion of separation.

Perceiving the manifest world as vibration in tune with the eternal rhythm of change is not knowledge possessed by the masses. Warriors are associated with thought vibrations of separation, so they are in the dense rhythm of worldly affairs. The sage knows nothing of this, having an evolved perception that visualizes the vibration of the ocean of consciousness in an eternal rhythm, which humbles the sage because it is divinely sublime. The warrior's mode of perception is bound by identity and involvement in the external world, while the sage sees the harmonious rhythm in all things. So in simplistic terms the warrior is fixed on duality and the sage sees the interdependent unity of all things, which is a non-dual state of consciousness. The manifest world then exists in two totally different ways to the two modes of being. A warrior believes life begins and ends in a linear fashion in a created world, while the sage perceives a constant pattern of birth, growth, decay, death, and rebirth or renewal in cycles with no beginning or ending.

THE ROLE OF ATTACHMENT

Most of us believe all things start and finish. We see birth and death within the world and believe these events are beginnings and endings in themselves. This is an amazing peculiarity, for, if the universe is unending and eternal, could there ever be a beginning or ending? The answer must surely be no, because if the physical and mental planes are governed by the eternal principles of rhythm and vibration, then that which they constitute cannot be finite. The manifest world is instead an eternal ocean of consciousness in motion with waves coming and going.

The masses believe in a beginning and an end because most beings live within the body-mind state of consciousness. In knowing only the world of form, they develop attachments. These attachments are usually to other human beings, but in some cases attachments develop with animals, plants, minerals, and material objects. All of these attachments serve to block the growth of consciousness within an individual. They blur the ability to see reality as it truly is. For those who are bound to the myriad world of forms, the song of the universe is incomprehensible. If no true knowledge exists, the dependence on attachments increases, which gives birth to desires and judgments. So the emotional attachment to anything serves as a hindrance to enlightenment. It is not that emotions are in any way wrong, but being overly attached to an emotional state identified with anything, robs us of our ability to change. The eternally formless has become a concrete form. For example, we may associate certain emotions with an individual; then, when that individual begins to change, our emotions become conflicted. In the same way the relationship between an individual and God is commonly misunderstood, with the ignorant blaming God for not complying with their ego's wants. All of this leads to anger, aggression, and hatred toward the individual or God for not complying with our emotional attachments.

Emotional attachments to anything bind us to our ego and sustain our perception of the universe in a narrow mold. Emotional attachments are the crux of why we believe in a beginning and an end. Our identification of emotions with any particular thing locks us into the details of life. For example, when there is the birth of a child, a natural joy is experienced because of the deep knowing that another soul has entered the world, but this joy is negated when the happiness is bound by the ego and attached to the birth experience. As this attachment develops over time, parents often continue to look back at the event of the birth, while not appreciating the child here and now.

As children grow they begin to develop their own level of awareness, which often goes against their parents' idea of who their child should be. This will cause years of friction as the parents' attachment prevents them from recognizing that their child is growing naturally as they need to. Later, when the child becomes a teenager and then a young adult, there is usually a time of reconciliation between child and parents. So the emotional attachment gets stronger. In its truest sense this is a beautiful thing. But say for instance fate steps in and the child who has grown into a thirty-three-year-old adult dies unexpectedly. The emotional attachment from the parents to their child is severed, so they begin to suffer. They believe that what they are attached to has been taken away from them. They begin to be drawn into the experience of the death of their child. Because they have only an understanding of the outer form, they erroneously believe that death was an ending. So they visualize their child's whole life in a process that began and ended. The emotional attachment has pulled them into the details of their child's life, and prevented them from seeing the unfoldment and pattern of that life.

A sage, on the other hand, sees the same event a different way. Knowing that the child has not gone anywhere, the sage would know it is absurd to suffer because of such an unfortunate event. A sage sees the universe from an elevated view and is thus able to intuit the universal breath of life. Being fixed in the spiri-

tual plane, the sage sees the physical and mental world as a phenomenon that rises and falls according to the process of change.
What a sage intuits is the propagation of vibration attuned to the
rhythm of the universe.

The wisdom of a sage knows that all beings within the universe come from the same source and return to the same source,
like a wave arising from and returning to the ocean. The sage sees
an individual as a wave always connected to the ocean, even if the
individual is not conscious of it. It is said that a wise man has a
smile on his face at a funeral, because he knows that even though
the body has died, the spirit within that body has just moved on
to a different experience according to the process of rhythm and
vibration.

THE RHYTHM OF THE VIBRATORY PULSE

The law of rhythm and vibration governs, constitutes, maintains,
and sustains the birth-death process of all living organisms within
the whole entire universe. These two eternal principles emanate
out of the spiritual plane and then into the mental, which then
creates the physical. As something moves back into the source,
the process is reversed from the physical to the spiritual. The
plant kingdom is a good reference for this cycle, because we can
see the constancy in plant life between the death of a plant and
the arrival of new plant life. Seen from above, the harmony in the
plant kingdom has a beautiful rhythm in tune with the seasons
and weather patterns, which enables plants to sustain a harmonious environment for other life-forms.

Nature has an intelligence that allows a planetary body to
remain in a constant rhythm. Minerals, plants, animals, and

humans all make up nature's rhythm and these four components benefit from one another. The perception of most human beings, however, is caught in the details; they do not focus on the ebb and flow of the natural world, so they ignorantly try to lord it over nature. A sage, on the other hand, sees all life, including humans, in a harmonious pattern of repetition.

The physical and mental planes are transient, but the vibratory pulse of the spiritual rhythm is eternal. The sage sees all living things as being in this universal pattern, which means the concept of birth and death must be an illusion. In the wisdom traditions this is explained through the concept of "reincarnation." To warriors reincarnation is absurd because they believe things begin and end. They do not understand how they are part of something eternal. If consciousness expands and contracts according to the eternal principles of rhythm and vibration, then reincarnation should be a logical fact. To assume that it isn't is to assume that human beings are outside of the universe. The conventional thoughts we have been indoctrinated with allow no space for reincarnation to conflict with our conditioned beliefs, even when a socially accepted institution such as science proves something as primal as reincarnation with pure logic and reason. The institution of science has gone even as far as revealing the primal relationships of thoughts, rhythm, and vibration in relationship to reincarnation. The genius scientist Walter Russell reveals these very connections in his remarkable treatise *A New Concept of the Universe*.

Idea is eternal. Bodies which manifest idea are transient but their repetitions are eternal. There is no exception to this process of repetitions of bodies which is called reincarnation when applied to man. The process is universal, however, and applies to all creating things—not man alone.

In Nature, one tone ceases to be and another becomes. In other words, one formula for a patterned wave vibration ceases when another measured vibration begins. We must also carry this thought farther by not thinking of cessations, beginnings and endings. We must think of them as awakened continuities which we can "put to sleep" when we have no further need of them, or "awaken" when we have need of them.

As Nature unfolds from the seed to record its patterns in moving body forms, it simultaneously refolds into its seed in order that the refoldings can be repeated in like patterns.[2]

Nothing can escape the law of change, so humans in their process of unfoldment rise and fall, only to rise again in a different form. Those who dwell only on the physical and mental planes do not see reality like this; they are bound to their emotional and material attachments to people and other things. The sage has a direct link to the Divine and can see the splendor in the universal unfoldment, no matter how grotesque some parts may appear to be. Sages are in sync with the rhythm of the universe, which allows all the forces of the cosmos to work through them, expressed as dharma. Dharma is the rhythm and vibration of the universe in the manifest through an individual's connection with the Divine Will.

Those who are sincere in the great work of eternity need to reintegrate themselves with the rhythm and vibration of the universe. This allows the individual to release the grip of identity and to harmonize with the formless substantial reality beyond the illusion of forms. In other words this would be a return to or union with the source. We find this return in Hindu mythology, which the label-less master Alan Watts explains beautifully in his eternal treatise *The Way of Zen*. *The Way of Zen* states:

> Fundamental to the life and thought of India from the very ear-
> liest times is the great mythological theme of *atma-yajna*—the
> act of "self-sacrifice" whereby God gives birth to the world, and
> whereby men, following the divine pattern, reintegrate them-
> selves with God. The act by which the world is created is the
> same act by which it is consummated—the giving up of one's
> life—as if the whole process of the universe were the type of
> game in which it is necessary to pass on the ball as soon as it is
> received. Thus the basic myth of Hinduism is that the world is
> God playing hide-and-seek with himself. As Prajapati, Vishnu,
> or Brahma, the Lord under many names creates the world by
> an act of self-dismemberment or self-forgetting, whereby the
> One becomes Many, and the single Actor plays innumerable
> parts. In the end, he comes again to himself only to begin the
> play once more—the One dying into the Many, and the Many
> dying into the One.[3]

The changing universe and the vibratory structure of creation cannot be changed to suit one's liking. Instead the key is to find out how these eternal attributes of the universe are within you as well. The sage knows they exist in all life-forms, so a sage con-templates the unification of all things. Watching the ocean of consciousness wave and crash, shine and gloom, a sage is unfazed. Seeing all life rise and fall, the sage knows that everything is always connected to the source. So where could there be room for suffering? One who is not emotionally or materially attached to anything does not suffer, having the ability to intuit the irreducible essence of the whole universe in all things.

This does not mean that a sage is above grieving; on the contrary there is always a time to grieve. The difference is that the sage doesn't grieve over a death but out of compassion for those who suffer. In the story of the parents and the child, a sage would not grieve for the departure of the child from this world, but would feel deeply for the parents. The evolution of perception does not mean becoming like a stone; on the contrary, it is having a heart open to all, through the vision of the harmonious rhythmic vibration in all manifest things. To a sage looking at anything is looking at oneself. Viewing the universe from the evolution of perception, a sage increasingly sees that nothing is separate; everything is part of an interdependent whole. This naturally manifests as the science of humility. The great work of eternity is to see that all aspects of consciousness are fundamentally one.

8
The Hypnosis of Duality

*T*he entire universe is an interdependent whole, a single being that includes every life-form. However, different perspectives of this universe arise from different identifications, which can be with the form or the formless. The form is the wave of identity existing in the physical and mental planes, while the formless is the ocean of consciousness existing in the spiritual plane. Viewed from an evolved state of consciousness, duality is transcended. As identity with the formless increases, the concept of separation fades. The eternal sage Chuang-tzu once said, "When there is no more separation between 'this' and 'that,' it is called the still-point of the Tao. At the still-point in the center of the circle one can see the infinite in all things."[1]

DEGREES OF DUALITY

Duality has its source within the thought vibrations of the mental plane. As we have already explained, the internal landscape of the mental world is reflected in the physical world. So all of the conditioning an individual undergoes from birth strengthens the illusion of separate things. The beliefs that bind us to our ego fracture our awareness so that we see disunity instead of harmony. Such beliefs are the foundation for all suffering and bloodshed in the universe. If duality is real then love must be untrue, because everything that comes from duality keeps us divided, with no understanding of one another. The common state of the masses is fear and hatred because of the illusion that each is separate from all other life in the universe. Insecurity stems from the idea that we are just the body-mind state of consciousness. This state of consciousness breeds a mentality of "us against them," with constant fear of an external attack, either physical or emotional.

Lacking awareness of the harmony playing out, individuals seek to further their existence by any means necessary, including harming others. Individuals living only on the physical and mental plane are perpetually caught in the details, either in their minds or what they see in the world of forms. They believe these apparent things are separate and finite. Not contemplating the origin of all things, they remain lost in the mental design of duality. The eternal essence of rhythm and vibration is not even within a warrior's comprehension, so it is impossible for them to understand that all life is connected in a unified field.

Duality is based on the theory that if you have good, then there must be bad, meaning that everything has its opposite. For example, we have the two poles of cold and hot, light and dark, being and non-being, microcosm and macrocosm, and so on. We know one cannot exist without the other; we need dark to know light, hot to know cold, and so on. Where does the light end and the dark begin? Does either have a definite ending or are they part of a continuous stream? All of these apparent opposites are in fact the same thing, differing only in degree. Just as a musical scale starts with C and moves up the scale in a continuous fashion until it reaches another C, the nature of duality between any two poles is an aspect of rhythm and vibration expressing itself in the manifest world.

In each area of consideration, such as good and bad or light and dark, the degree of separation between the poles is determined by an individual's psychology, which varies according to the individual's conditioning. When the masses see duality in the world, they are only trying to interpret the polarity they have created in their mind.

SEEING ALL AS ONE

These polarities hold an abstract key to real knowledge. The eternal sage Chuang-tzu stated that he could see the infinite in all things because his perception had let go of the so-called known and entered into the unknowable. In gaining experiential knowledge of the Tao, Chuang-tzu started to intuit what the eternal master Lao-tzu was describing or, we could say, not describing. In Lao-tzu's eternal scripture the *Tao Te Ching,* he explains duality from the perspective of the evolution of perception. Chapter 2 of the *Tao Te Ching* states:

> *When people see some things as beautiful,*
> *other things become ugly.*
> *When people see some things as good,*
> *other things become bad.*
> *Being and non-being create each other.*

Difficult and easy support each other.
Long and short define each other.
High and low depend on each other.
Before and after follow each other.
Therefore the Master
acts without doing anything
and teaches without saying anything.
Things arise and she lets them come;
things disappear and she lets them go.
She has but doesn't possess,
acts but doesn't expect.
When her work is done, she forgets it.
That is why it lasts forever.[2]

Watching the universe unfold in all its wonder, a sage perceives only the course of things rising and falling as one entity. As the sage's whole being is immersed in the spiritual plane, the perception that emanates through the mental and physical plane is the pure light of creation from the source. The sage perceives all as one on all levels of life. Even on the physical plane, objects are not seen as separate from one another; all coexist in one form.

To the masses all forms are solid objects moving around in space and time. Contemplation of the origin of all things is too hard to comprehend while clinging to a notion of a separate isolated ego. A sage on the other hand sees all forms functioning in unison, following the eternal modes of rhythm and vibration. All events of physical nature are in accordance with the harmony of the universe. Where there are wars, famine, senseless violence, chaos, and so on, a sage sees a process of unfoldment in perfect harmony. The sage is not wrapped up in emotional attachments to anything; thus the sage does not know death. The sage sees that all things return to the same source.

The physical world is an expression of pure consciousness, which is an artistic pattern of the eternal, so duality does not have its roots in the physical plane. The real sickness of duality exists in the illusions impressed upon the mind, not because of the form in the physical world. The mental plane of consciousness is a conduit between the physical and spiritual. What is projected from the mind usually has an emotional connection to the individual. The development of the psychological effect known as the ego causes the duality between forms. It is hard for most to shed this illusion because they do not know they are only acting out what they have learned. The great work of eternity is to comb out all latent tendencies and iron out all habitual ways (known as vasanas in Sanskrit), so the real "you" can stand before the world for the first time.

TRANSCENDING THE MIND

In most humans the whole structure of the mental plane is filled with egotistical noise. The thought vibrations are never settled because they are based on the mode of duality, which causes us to be incessantly chattering within our own mind. When we see someone talking to themselves, we typically think they are crazy, yet we are constantly talking to ourselves within our own minds. It is also craziness, only expressed within.

These unsteady thought vibrations are the result of a belief in separation constantly inculcated into all of us from the beginning of our reemergence into this world. Instead of searching for who we were before all of this conditioning, we have entrusted our faith in a ghost: the false ego. If what causes the idea of duality is false, then duality itself does not exist. Duality is only there because we have believed in our illusions. The mental plane has become congested with the noise of thought vibrations that maintain a world with no external peace. But the mental plane in its original structure is nothing like this. Rather, it is empty like space, which allows dharma to flow through the mind. This is a sage's consciousness, so they know that duality is mere illusion.

The duality existing within the mental framework is built on the premise that there is the false ego and the true self. The problem with this view is the fact that the ego does not exist. Many people who tread the path of spiritual cultivation make a common mistake in this view of their own mental framework—after identifying the ego chattering within their head, they set out to battle against it. Some arrogantly set out to transcend the mind, not realizing that nothing is more egotistic than that. This only aggravates the problem.

If we are to truly transcend the mind, then our mind needs to be fully open to allow the universe to flow through it. This is why dharma is the mental virtue of the spiritual world: dharma can only flow through the mind when it has regained its original purity, which is the eternal essence of space. Transcending the mind does not mean going above and beyond it; that would be the ego's way of arrogantly interpreting it. Transcending really means bringing the mind back to its pure state, that of an empty vessel. Transcending the mind means to empty out the mind to reestablish the connection with the spiritual plane. In an empty or open mind, duality ceases to be. All apparent opposites, both within and without, dissolve.

Even the distinction between the false ego and the true self disappears from the awareness of a sage. Most people do not realize this when they continue their own spiritual introspection, because they begin to overanalyze what's going on within. In the end distinguishing between the ego and the true self is still duality. A sage, on the other hand, refines consciousness into a single point, which transforms her into the complete state. To be holy is to become a whole being in direct connection with the Absolute, where duality could not exist. The sage knows that the more we overanalyze, the more we are caught in the illusion of duality. To a self-realized sage the ego is nothing more than a mirage; because it doesn't really exist, it poses no problem for a sage. The ego becomes like a distant background noise, much like a neighbor playing some music far off in the distance. As the sage enters the center more and more, even the background noise tapers off into silence.

A sage confirms to her disciples that there is only the true self. The problem is that we each need to realize this for ourselves; a sage can only point us in the right direction. But most of us are still under the spell of the ego, which is a potent combination of beliefs, conditioning, emotional attachments, and thoughts, an accumulation of our past experience. A sage sees all of that as part of the phenomenal world. The deluded individual identifies with thoughts rather than the thinker of the thoughts. One who is sincere in the great work of eternity comes to know that thoughts come and go, so to be moved by thoughts is much like someone who is dominated by an external threat. But the truth is that we are only dominated by an internal threat: the power we attribute to the illusory ego.

The majority of thought vibrations are associated with the individual's conditioning, rather than being pure thought originating from the spiritual plane. This is why dharma is so scarce.

If the mind is empty, then the expression of the pure thought from the spiritual plane as dharma becomes common. This is known only to a sage who is capable of perceiving the universe through the eyes of non-dual consciousness. Sages do not perceive thoughts as something belonging to them; instead their awareness of thoughts is exactly the same as their perceptions of the physical world.

The rising and falling of thought vibrations is reflected by the physical world. As we mentioned the mental creates the physical. The empty mind can be seen in the reflection of nature, while the deluded mind is found in the human element of chaos. It depends on where our perception is rooted. Most of us do not see that thoughts are rising and falling, so we only contribute to chaos and entropy. The sage, on the other hand, perceives eternity in all things while remaining in the center. Thoughts are regarded as bubbles of the mind, which will soon burst. Just as a sage watches the rhythm and vibrations of the physical world, so does she watch the rhythm and vibrations of the mental world. Thoughts are nothing but waves of the mind. Most choose to ride the wave, while the sage has sunk down into the non-dual ocean. Diving head first into the eternal universe, the sage finds all things in harmony in relation to the laws of rhythm and vibration.

OVERCOMING THE DELUSION OF INTERNAL AND EXTERNAL

The notion that separation exists in this universe is only an opinion of the deluded mind. A warrior dissects all things into two and then many without seeing what is fundamentally obvious. This leads to the ultimate duality. Even those who are seeking enlightenment get caught in the trap of analyzing themselves in the categories of two worlds, the external and the internal. Many who embark on the journey of self-realization and transformation are deceived by this last remnant of duality, because they do not see themselves in the external landscape. Not seeing the physical world as a mirror of the mental plane, they seek to disappear from it. But their belief that they need to retreat from the external world or even the mind means they are still under the illusion that separation is real.

The illusion of separation is not found in the consciousness of a sage, no matter what that duality is. The evolution of perception is a very different awareness of the universe than those still under the spell of worldly affairs. Nothing could exist as dual for a sage, not even within and without. A sage sees only the law of eternity in all things. Within and without collapse in on each other due to the fundamental laws of rhythm and vibration. The world arises as vibration from the source and then returns. All components of consciousness are in the universal flow, so to the sage the universe is just vibration in a rhythm of a divine tune, a song without words. When neither the within nor the without exist, then reality is seen for the first time. The utterings of the eternal sage Dattatreya, which became the eternal treatise *Song of the Avadhut,* explain this merging of all worlds into the reality of non-duality. Chapter 3, verse 18 reads:

> *I'm beyond both division and non-division;*
> *I'm the absolute reality.*
>
> *Within? Without? How could I be? I'm the*
> *absolute reality.*

I was never created; I'm not an object with
substance.

I'm nectarean knowledge, unchanging bliss;
I'm everywhere, like space.[3]

A sage can confirm that there is no within or without because to him all is one. This can be true for any of us if we are sincere in finding out who we truly are. Watching the universe unfold, a sage is comforted, because he knows he is one with the cosmos. Observing life rise and fall and knowing duality could not exist anywhere is the complete state. The sage sees the universe always as part of himself with no concept of within or without. His perception is attuned to the breath of the Absolute, where the exhalation vibrates things into existence in a flow of rhythm and the inhalation returns all vibration back to rest with the source. No one is separate from this process.

The masses unknowingly try to swim against the eternal current and thereby live a life of frustration and struggle. Holding on to their conditioning, they try to force the world to their own will. A sage holds on to nothing and thus unlearns everything, to just be as the universe is. When all these layers of learning fall away, then the evolution of perception has been fully actualized and lived. This state is what leads one to the mystical nondual consciousness of a sage. Things cease to be separate objects and there are no longer any thoughts associated with things. All apparent things are connected and one with the consciousness of the sage. Having embodied the whole universe, the sage is flowing as one with it. This is what it means to be in harmony with the Tao, or to be one with Brahman, God, Allah, the Absolute, and so on. Having assimilated all aspects of consciousness, a sage brings the mysterious science of humility forward. Only one thing stands in the way of seeing through the eyes of Brahman, and that is the power and illusion of maya.

MAYA'S DIRTY WINDOW

That which traps us in the hypnosis of duality is termed *maya* in Sanskrit. Maya refers to the world of illusion, which in this case is separation. This is a broad description, as English is sometimes an inadequate language for translating Sanskrit words; in fact maya is much more subtle. The involution of the cosmic breath is that perception that gets caught in the details. The illusion of maya is how we dissect things into separate parts.

A sage, as we have discussed, does not see separate things but instead perceives an inseparable whole. In this enlightened position, the sage fragments the light of the spiritual plane through the crystal clear prism of the mind or mental plane. Those who are under the spell of maya attempt to fragment that same spiritual light through the prism of their minds, which are clouded by their beliefs, like a dirty glass window that blocks the full light of the sun. Nature is innocent and springs from the same source as human life; the illusion is our mind that splits one universe into separate parts.

Maya comes from the Sanskrit root word *matr*, which means "to measure, build, define, form or lay out a plan of structure." Matr is the source of the Greco-Latin words *material, matrix, matter,* and *meter.* So maya is "the illusion of measuring something immeasurable." The measuring of life is the ego swept up in the details of reality. The illness of humankind is therefore the measurement of things into separate parts. We have this tendency to want to describe every little thing we see, which in the end isolates us from the whole. No one ever asks why we define things, because the answer is too shocking for those with less knowledge. We have an addiction to trying to describe things because we want to control everything, no matter how absurd that control may be. The whole game of maya is that we project separation on to nature. We constantly want to lord it over nature, because we don't understand it. Our conventional thoughts measure nature so we can feel it corresponds to what we believe. This is the result of mass hypnosis.

Nature itself is innocent; it moves in relation to the divine rhythm of the universe. The majority of humans on this planet have lost their innocence because they believe they are separate from nature. The more we try to project our ideas on nature, which is at the fountainhead of the source, the more we are closing this chapter known as the human species. The controlling aspect of human life is wound up in the insecurity of the individual. Chaos exists because our individual internal landscapes are out of control. They are out of control because we are attempting to control life, which is in truth uncontrollable.

When we look within our own being, we find the thought vibrations moving of their own accord, likewise with nature. As we grow we attach to the thought vibrations that build the ego. Then, as we become more aware, we seek to control the ego without the full knowledge that it doesn't exist. Trying to control something ephemeral is a prime symptom of internal duality. Believing that we have two sides is as common a mistake as believing there is a within and a without. This is perfectly normal; those who realize they are not their conditioning would obviously want to rid themselves of the clutches of the ego. But the problem arises from the attempt to take over the ego by controlling it, instead of just letting it go completely. This control that most individuals harbor is part of the conditioning interwoven in the illusionary garment of the ego.

MEASURING MAYA THROUGH THE PAIN OF PLEASURE

Whenever we are measuring, we are under the influence of maya. Not being in the position of a sage who just observes, we find ourselves analyzing whether something is good or bad. Perceiving the ego as bad still binds one to duality and the power of maya. The urge to control is born from being lost in the details of life.

One of our grand attempts to control the universe has been the imposition of a man-made calculation of time on that which is timeless. Not understanding the rhythm and vibration of the cosmos, we project our mind and try to measure the eternal. This began a long time ago with ancient systems such as astrology, which was a more mysterious way of measuring the universe than what the modern era has produced. Time is increasingly becoming more of a mechanical system, reflecting civilization's growing intellect and dying intuition. It is the height of arrogance to try to push the universe around to be convenient for our own life. Our version of time is an attempt to tell the universe how it is. Time is only useful to the world of maya and all its illusionary separate parts.

Time is only one of many indications that we crave control and have the absurd idea that we can measure something immeasurable. All things that are measured are in the field of duality; nothing can be excluded from this. An enlightened sage has no sense of measurement. The sage realizes that trying to control something is like a knife trying to cut itself; it just can't be done. The consciousness of a sage is so different from intellectual reasoning that in the eyes of the profane it is incomprehensible. The eternal treatise of India known as the *Mandukya Upanishad* illustrates this immeasurable way beyond maya.

> (It is) That which is conscious neither of the subjective nor of the objective, nor of both; which is neither simple consciousness, nor undifferentiated sentience, nor mere darkness. It is unseen, without relations, incomprehensible, uninferable, and indescribable— the essence of Self-consciousness, the ending of *maya*.[4]

Maya's focus of attention on the illusion of separate things breeds fear in the human psyche. Fear itself is not our enemy because it acts as a guide for us to become more humble. The problem is that we do not want to have or feel any fear or pain, so we try to control it by seeking pleasure. But this type of control is based on duality, on the belief that pain and pleasure exist as separate feelings. As we have explained, two opposite poles are actually identical in nature. So pain and fear can only exist if we believe in pleasure, and vice versa. If we knew that fear was something to embrace rather than loathe, neither pain nor pleasure could have a grip on us. Instead, our pursuit of pleasure only enhances the influence of pain because we have bought into the illusion that they exist as two separate feelings. We identify with pleasure either physically or mentally and try to hold on to what is pleasurable according to the ego without allowing pain to exist. This contributes to the suffering experienced in this world either physically or emotionally.

The measurement of maya begins within an individual and then extends out into the collective. The pursuit of pleasure for an individual becomes the pursuit of pleasure for a nation, a religion, a race, and a gender. These four core pillars of separation are mere mental constructs. When individuals identify pleasure in association with a nation, a religion, a race, and a gender, they then attempt to maintain these constructs by any means necessary. War, famine, senseless violence, and other tragedies are all spawned by this ignorant attitude toward pleasure and pain. Clinging to what our individual and collective egos deem a pleasurable way of life causes not only nature to suffer, but also other people on this planet. The irony of trying to hold on to what we believe is pleasure is that we will constantly experience pain in life. Suffering cannot be overcome from a warrior's perception. In this mode of being, the individual and the collective both suffer from the individual's hypnosis.

Pursuing only pleasure causes anxiety because we see that the so-called pleasurable moments in life don't last. So we engage in a constant pursuit of pleasurable experiences, not realizing that every time we do this, the pendulum will swing back harder and harder to the pole of pain. All of these are nothing more than the waves of vibration that we identify with. If we could truly see the universe in its rising and falling nature, then we would never attempt to measure and control reality. Maya only exists because we are still trying to control everything; in this state fear is naturally a part of our existence. We are forcing ourselves upon the universe instead of flowing with it. Our belief that we are outside of the universe and our lack of trust in how the universe is unfolding are both neurotic.

Suffering in any form exists because we have this absurd idea that we can control the rhythm and vibrations of the universe. When we see reality beyond the eyes of maya, we find that we are inseparable from the harmony of the universe. The evolution of perception of a sage is the ultimate remedy for our deluded view of the universe and all forms of suffering. In not attempting to control any aspect of life, be it pain and pleasure, or another human or nature, a sage allows the universe to take its course without clutching to anything.

The evolution of perception is not some cold awareness that feels no empathy for life. On the contrary, a sage has an immense empathy for the universe, which expresses itself as immeasurable compassion for all life. A sage knows that the root of all suffering is seeing all as separate, resulting in efforts to control reality. Knowing the universe is unceasing in its rhythm, the sage recognizes that the audacious attempt to control the events of the universe is a battle that can never be won. One who is sincerely humble will flow with the stream and become one with it, while those who attempt to impose their will on the universe will continue to suffer. The evolution of perception grants the vision that the universe is happening to us rather than we to it. Naturally this understanding leads to the science of humility.

9
Now Is the House of Spontaneity

As the universe happens to us, we can be conscious of it or remain ignorant of it. Those who are conscious are devoted to the universe in a similar sense that a religious individual is devoted to their idea of God. Devotion in the truest sense is the reverence of the individual being, the microcosm, for the universal, the macrocosm. Such devotion to the universe initiates access to the suppressed feminine energy of the cosmos. For ages the entire population has been developing the masculine force of energy; if we continue to express only this part of consciousness, then our planet will come to a fiery end, as fire is the element associated with the masculine.

However, water, the most humble force in nature, can extinguish fire. Water, associated with the feminine principle of the universe, always seeks the lowest point and moves without form. As water moves down a mountain stream, the water cannot be shaped and is not attached to the land it travels over, which allows its movement. Another example of water is a cloud in relation to a mountain. The eternal sage Tung-shan Liang-chieh (in Chinese), also known in Japanese as Tozan Ryokai, once said,

> The blue mountain is father of the white cloud. The white cloud is the son of the blue mountain. All day long they depend on each other, without being dependent on each other. The white cloud is always the white cloud. The blue mountain is always the blue mountain.[1]

If we see ourselves as the white cloud, we can intuitively understand our relationship to the universe and how it continues to mold us in its rhythm. Our existence is both independent and dependent. When conditions change for the white cloud, it just changes and keeps moving. If we allow the universe to happen to us in this fashion, the essence of the universe will begin to shine through our consciousness.

When we truly trust the universe and allow the course of things to flow, we become a receiver of the cosmos. This means not arguing with our circumstances in life, no matter how painful they are. This is a hard state of awareness for most to truly embrace, yet it is imperative in the growth of our consciousness. If we are sincere in the great work of eternity, we must persevere with this way of being receptive to life. Even when we know this intellectually, we might try to justify the input of our egos into the details, leading us to fall back into the trap of trying to impose our will on the universe. This implies a lack of trust in the design.

When we consider our physical body, we realize that we do not need to think for every cell or make our liver operate correctly. We have an inbuilt knowing that all the parts of our physical organism will work in harmony. It would be ridiculous to try to force our liver to function in a particular way or to tell our cells to stop their infighting. If this is obviously ridiculous on the level of the human body, why is it not on a universal level? The fact that we don't trust the universe in the same way as we trust our internal organs is a prime example of our unnecessary struggle for control of life. This comes back to the body-mind state of consciousness. Those who believe they are only the body that houses the mind experience fear; the wish to control the outside world is born of obvious insecurity.

Suffering is maintained by the concept that we are only the body-mind state, because we fear the spontaneity of the cosmos. But we cannot avoid the way the universe is happening to us. The idea that we can control anything vanishes from the awareness of those who are sincere in the great work of eternity. Humility is the virtue of truly receiving life with an unwavering gratitude toward existence. But this is not how we are taught to be in this world. The pervasive ignorance of who we truly are has spawned a perpetual chain of hypnotized teachers.

CONSCIOUS RECEIVING

The spontaneity of life can never be destroyed, so being a conscious receiver of the cosmos should be a logical conclusion. We all receive food that nourishes our internal organs. We do not force our food to accomplish this; we just receive the food and trust that it will nourish the body, and it does. We need to extend that same trust to our experiences. As the constant nourishment of food allows us to grow and be healthy, so does the constant nourishment of experience allow our consciousness to grow and be healthy. Physical nourishment and universal nourishment function in the same way: they both begin with trust. The spontaneity of experience constantly dished up by the universe is the nourishment our soul needs to deepen its connection with the source.

The ability to observe that the universe is just happening allows us to open up fully to spontaneous experience. The receptive aspect of the universe is the feminine humility. Many sacred texts such as the *I Ching* teach that the receptive principle allows the universe to take its course on all levels without hampering its rhythm. We move in relation to the universe, not the other way around. Being receptive we learn through our own direct experience that we are a reflection of the cosmos, not just metaphorically, but as the actual microcosm of the All. In most wisdom traditions human as microcosm of the macrocosm is a foundational revelation, yet this is only the merging of opposites that are identical in nature. The esoteric meaning behind the merging of apparent opposites is that the individual goes from being the microcosm to becoming the macrocosm. *Human as macrocosm* is the occult knowledge possessed by one in this state. This again is nothing more than the evolution of perception in a different context.

The result of this way of being is complete receptivity. All experiences are taken as lessons to aid one's growth until enlightenment is realized. The non-dual state of consciousness that is referred to as nirvana, samadhi, satori, and enlightenment can only be realized by those who have become receivers of the universe. Understanding the knowledge of the three planes of consciousness, they can see their internal world in the external landscape through the experiences that reflect their thought vibrations.

Those with less knowledge continue to fight their experiences, not realizing that those reflections of themselves are what they asked for, which they may need to grow. The enlightened view is that experience is spontaneous and unavoidable. A sage who sees through these eyes is aware that there is no within or without and thus lets go completely. Otherwise it is like fighting your own existence while trying to prevent your own life from happening. The way or path for one who is able to again and again let go and receive becomes increasingly free of obstacles; it will flow without any unexpected snags along the way. For those who no longer hold on to any thoughts or conditioned projections of things, life becomes a living art form. As the conditioned beliefs about the world are dissolved, we begin to experience who we truly are.

Taking part in the great work of eternity is a constant enquiry into the reality we create individually and collectively. Sometimes an experience is so convincing that we are drawn into the drama of the mind. As the situation cannot be controlled, we can receive the experience in all humility and then digest it. The more receptive we are, the deeper and more profound the insights will be. Receiving the universe as it happens is a relinquishment of all quests; this is a key ingredient in true and authentic liberation.

A PUZZLING QUESTION

Realizing that this universe goes on no matter what we think gives rise to a very puzzling question. Is this universe happening to me or am I happening to it? Asking such a question may seem absurd to the less enlightened, yet this question reveals the utter duplicity of all life. Being receptive reveals that our own existence is only happening in accord with the cosmos. As the label-less master Alan Watts once asked, "Do you do it, or does it do you?"[2]

Such a question is as puzzling as trying to explain why we exist. The only way we can enquire into such a question is to understand our relationship to the totality of the universe. If we are the microcosm of the universe and not separate from it, then it is not the universe "doing" us, nor are we "doing" the universe, because both are inseparable. It is all happening together as one.

As we mentioned a physical organism receives its food and experience on an individual level, which is a reflection of nourishment on a universal scale. The universe receives all experiences without objection or judgment. It allows all phenomena to take place within its infinite space. From the universal perspective all rhythm, vibration, and the manifest world come into existence from empty space. Even the primal energy of the universe emerges from this empty Void. To know why the manifest world exists is tantamount to understanding why space holds it together; some things just cannot be known on a human level. To attempt to know such things is to miss the point, because what we try to intellectualize is so simple. As a matter of fact, it is as simple as space.

The challenge for one in the human body is to realize the formless substantial reality within the world of forms. Even though that may appear simple to the intellect, most do not truly understand it because if they did then they would renounce all worldly quests. The great work of eternity is about truthfully assimilating this knowledge, becoming capable of perceiving the formless in all life in its movements of rhythm and vibration from the source. All the parts of the manifest world are like one big wave that comes into existence from the ocean of nothingness.

A good analogy for this interconnected happening is sound. Silence is comparable with space and sound with the wave of the manifest world. Where does sound arise from? Is sound independent? These questions lead to the realization that sound cannot exist without silence. Sound emerges out of silence and then returns to silence, but this is only half true, because sound can only come out of the present moment. Where, then, do the sounds of the past exist? They exist as echoes within the matrix of our mind. Sound comes out of "now," and we make the "now" moment echo through our memory. Silence, then, does not exist in the past or the future; it exists in the now and is of the now. Silence, like space, is ever present, because silence is only now and can be nowhere else.

Sound offers a key illustration of our interconnected relationship to the universe. Like sound, we come into existence from space, which has no limitation. If we identify with the world of form, then we have bought into the illusion of maya. Limitation is projected from the mind upon the belief in separate parts. We cannot have the manifest world without space. This being the case, the manifest world is arising out of space. All the laws that constitute and govern the manifest universe are like the frequency of sound that comes into existence and then trails off into silence. Rhythm and vibration rise and fall in relation to the empty Void. All phenomena move and exist in relation to space. Space itself is boundless and infinite, with no past or future. Space cannot be heard, thus it is silence, which only exists now. Like sound in silence, life in space cannot exist anywhere else but now. If anything is not in the now, then it is a mere phantom. When we are receptive to the interconnected happening of reality and can intuit its harmony, then we are witnesses to the space that exists in all things, which can only be now.

Even the concept of having a creator or being part of a creation doesn't exist, as consciousness cannot be anywhere else but in the Eternal Now. To look so far into the past, one would again be under the spell of maya and not in the Eternal Now. Being receptive allows the spontaneity of the universe to take place; it is becoming empty like space with no attachments to this and that. It means simply observing the universe and allowing the cosmos to take its course without interfering with it. When we realize that space holds the universe together and consciousness is that, then the ocean of the source will enter our being more and more. The more receptive we are, the more eternity will transform us into what religion calls "the image of God" or what is known in occult wisdom as the human as macrocosm. In this transformation we do not become God, but instead are liberated from the concept of God and the illusion of separation.

When interpreted by our mind, our lives are like echoes in empty space, yet how could our life echo if there is no past or future? In the Eternal Now we are as much space as form because the formless is our origin. This is expressed by two Taoist sayings, "What do we value most, the cup, or the space within the cup?" and, "What is more valuable, the walls of a house, or the space within the walls?" So which are you? The one the universe is happening to? Or the one who is the witness of it? The one who perceives it is in the Eternal Now, because there is no one that the universe is happening to, and the echoes of the mental plane have dissolved into silence. This is the revered state of enlightenment, when we verify how the universe actually exists through our own being. If there is only the Eternal Now, then the universe is that which expresses itself as spontaneity.

10

At the Center of the Universe Is a Jivanmukta

❧

Jivanmukta is the Sanskrit word for one who is completely liberated in this life, one who has entered the revered state of moksha, nirvana, samadhi, satori, and enlightenment. A sage's ultimate realization should be that of a jivanmukta, one capable of leading others to freedom. In receiving the whole universe, a jivanmukta becomes a light-giver for this world.

The jivanmukta reveals what is termed a "solar body" in the context of traditional esoteric knowledge, while one who is seeking knowledge is said to possess a "lunar body." The sun is the giver of light and the moon is the receiver of light. Similarly, the sage or jivanmukta is the human reflection of the sun, and the masses are the human reflection of the moon. The light we are speaking of is the unfathomable and unknowable essence of the source shining through our beingness. The light-giving source on the human level is eternal knowledge and wisdom. This knowledge and wisdom isn't conventional; it exists in the experiential realm of deeply profound introspection. A jivanmukta has renounced all worldly quests and projections on the universe to become a channel for eternity to manifest itself.

The receptive principle of the universe aligns the jivanmukta to the source underlying all things. Thus rooted in the Eternal Now, the jivanmukta flows in unison with the harmonic course of the cosmos. The evolution of perception is to see things as they are in truth, which allows the jivanmukta to be completely humble to the entire universe, with no need to force the universe's hand to suit any psychological state. This is not easily understood and can be used to mislead the spiritually starved.

A jivanmukta knows that controlling or attempting to control anything, whether physically, mentally, or spiritually, is in the field of duality. Those who consciously attempt to create or co-create are still under the spell of maya, believing that their psychology is separate from the environment. They are choosing to impose their will on the environment to suit their beliefs about how the world should be. This phenomenon has resulted in an inauthentic comprehension of the law of attraction and mental alchemy. Individuals who are focused on something they want for themselves and the world, or groups trying to consciously co-create for the same reason, both generate delusional egotistic projections. To consciously create or co-create means being possessed by judgments and desires that are the result of false perceptions. It is not that creativity is a bad thing, but creation is not natural when individuals attempt to force their opinion of life upon the universe.

The law of attraction, mental alchemy, and dharma are not esoteric sciences for us to learn so that we can apply them to the universe. On the contrary, they are the virtues of eternity that flow through the consciousness of an individual, which we have put into an intellectual landscape. Superficial understandings have misled many throughout time and especially within the modern era. Truth is not something we can create or co-create. That is absurd. If you are trying to consciously create or co-create a better world, you have missed the point. While it is possible for some to create their reality to suit their own lives, it will not lead to liberation. It simply proves that they have not let go of life and therefore can never be one with the irreducible essence of the universe. Most people don't want to let go because they want the universe to correspond with their beliefs.

Anyone can witness another's spiritual inauthenticity when they express their view of the world through the psychic filters of nation, religion, race, and gender. Dharma has nothing to do with such projections, as it is a virtue that flows through an empty mind. Mental alchemy functions in this fashion, not in the fashion of forcing oneself upon the universe. The relinquishment of one's individual will to reveal a soul is not something accomplished by creating or co-creating, but rather by letting go of all ideas of creating a so-called better world to suit oneself.

Some may say this appears to be an anti-humanist perspective of the world, but this is mere ignorance. The only way we can become truly human is to be guided by the essence of our being, which is humility, the expression of the receptive. True anti-humanism is having an agenda for the world based on our own conditioning. This is why movements to create a better world, with slogans such as "create your own reality" or "conscious co-creation," fall short of the mark. We must receive first and then create, not the other way around. Unfortunately, the masses interpret this as being completely passive. This is another form of spiritual inauthenticity.

The creative aspect of our being is most beautiful when dharma is expressed, but this can only be so if we are completely receptive. True conscious co-creation happens when the individual has aligned with the feminine receptivity of the universe. Agendaless beings will create a new world free of suffering through their own evolution, not the other way around. True freedom or liberation has nothing to do with the external world being at peace. To be meaningful all external stimuli need to be subject to our own introspection. While jivanmuktas are completely receptive to the universe, they are not influenced by the external world in any way.

One of the biggest traps of spiritual cultivation is to arm yourself with a lot of information, thinking that this will lead you to freedom. But nothing of a separate nature can be the source of liberation. Information can help mold your character or point you in a different direction, but in the end it also needs to be let go of. Information is only concepts and ideas of thoughts. When you deepen your perception of the universe, you discover that information is nothing to be taken seriously, as it is transient. Information itself rises and falls without leaving a trace. The science of humility is beyond words and cannot be pointed to by any information conceivable. Eternity cannot be grasped by information; it can only be experienced. For a sage information loses its appeal, as it has nothing to do with the only reality of the Eternal Now. The ultimate state is beyond anything we can conceive of; that universal spontaneity can only be experienced in the mystery of the breath of Brahma.

SADHANA

The human psyche always wants to achieve something through work toward a particular goal. Not being receptive to the universe, we want to force our enlightenment through a constant practice of various forms of spiritual cultivation, known in Sanskrit as *sadhana*. The ego is always looking into the past and the future to achieve something by suffering for it. But the concept of suffering to gain is an intellectual standpoint of the grossly conditioned. We believe in accumulating information to become smarter and more knowledgeable than others. But the accumulation of more and more information only enhances the conditioning to a point where we become proud of our intellect. In most cases such excessive knowledge and information can serve to distract us from whatever we are trying to comprehend.

This also can be the case for the great work of eternity. Those who are seeking enlightenment through a regimented practice are trying to control their experience to gain the so-called reward of enlightenment. This concept of practice and rewards pulls them away from the universal reality of spontaneity. The trap of the ego is the belief that some form of practice will grant them control over their life. This includes trying to gain control through some form of spiritual cultivation, such as the physical practice of yoga called Hatha Yoga. Those who practice Hatha Yoga become more aware of the subtle energies within their body that are called *prana* in Sanskrit and *chi* or *qi* in Chinese. Hatha Yoga brings this about by stretching the body, as this allows the meridian lines of the body to open and energy to flow through them freely, which stabilizes the mental vibrations. The purpose of Hatha Yoga is to realize this energy and thus to develop a connection with the higher planes of consciousness.

In the yoga system there are many forms or levels of yoga. Hatha Yoga is the beginning point, which sets one in motion toward the higher realizations of Raja Yoga (Royal Yoga), Dhyana Yoga (Yoga of Wisdom), which is expressed also as Jnana or Gnani, and then Bhakti Yoga (Yoga of God). Those who reach the enlightened state of a dhyana yogi or a bhakti yogi usually realize they were always in union with God; a wry smile comes to the face of those who sees that all their practice in the search for enlightenment was futile. The word *yoga* itself comes from the root Sanskrit word *yug,* which means "to join" or "union with God." *Tat tvam asi* in Sanskrit, which means "That Art Thou," refers to this eternal union. The idea that we can *practice* yoga is absurd, because we are "That" now.

Yoga refers to the reality of spontaneity in the universe found in the Eternal Now. There is nowhere to go, nothing to practice. The intellect finds this hard to fathom, as it is built on the assumption that we need to suffer to achieve something, while not believing that we can be worthy now without any effort. One reason for this is that the intellect is a forcing principle of the mind. More often than not, it is out of coherence with our receptive nature. In this way we try to force enlightenment upon ourselves through a stern form of spiritual cultivation. We are then perpetually our own worst enemies, as we are the ones in our own way from realizing that we are "That" now.

We cannot practice to be receptive and spontaneous, as these are both revelations of the evolution of perception. Only when we have the eyes of the evolution of perception does it dawn on us that there was actually nothing to do to reach enlightenment.

The spontaneous universe is us; if we know that, there is only the Eternal Now and nothing else. But few of us feel this, because we have had constant conditioning since birth, which deludes us into believing maya is real. If we are heavily conditioned, we face a peculiar dilemma in the face of a spontaneous universe; if we are subject to strong vasanas (latent tendencies and conditioned habits), we will never accept that we are worthy of realizing enlightenment so simply. We foolishly want to suffer to feel worthy. Then a sage would direct us to rigorous practice to expel a lot of our strong identity. This would be so even if we intellectually know that we are already one with the source.

Practice can be a necessary tool for us to loosen our grip of identity to sink deeper into the ocean of consciousness. Many forms of spiritual cultivation are useful in helping us to become more silent and centered beings. Practice then can be seen as a beautiful process of unfoldment that tames any character, no matter how strong the conditioning. But the forcing way of practice can only take our unfoldment so far. It will prepare us to take the next steps into the higher states of consciousness, but not into the mysterious world of moksha, nirvana, samadhi, satori, and enlightenment. As the eternal sage Lin Chi once said, "If a man seeks the Buddha, that man loses the Buddha."[1]

NIRVANA AND SAMSARA

Nirvana is the Sanskrit word used in Buddhism for the complete state, or one who has transcended the details of the world, or we could say transcended maya, into the enlightened mastery of a jivanmukta. Most wisdom traditions do not have a good grasp on what nirvana is and how it is embodied. As a result nirvana is sometimes mistakenly seen as some sort of goal to reach or something one can practice to gain. Most beings who seek nirvana undertake some form of sadhana to reach it. In this view the illusion of maya has tricked the individual into the field of duality. Nirvana is viewed as something separate from the universe, but nirvana is the complete state, a non-dual state of consciousness, which has no concept of distinction within it.

The word *nirvana* itself refers to non-duality; one who has this consciousness does not know what we call nirvana because they are That. As soon as we define *nirvana* or enlightenment as something to reach, we have missed the point. Even Buddha himself had this realization. After seven years of thorough asceticism, Gautama the Buddha finally accepted a bowl of some sort of milky soup from a girl looking after cattle and in doing so broke his strict discipline of asceticism. He simply gave up. Completely relieved, Gautama the Buddha sat under the Bodhi tree with the burden of seeking enlightenment lifted. He realized that he had not completely let go of life and was trying to force enlightenment upon himself. That night Gautama the Buddha realized that what we are ultimately after is not found in an attempt to transcend this world; enlightenment is actually found in the duplicity of life.

If our focus is on enlightenment or transcendence, then we are again caught in the detail of life. When we pursue our own form of spiritual cultivation, we erroneously believe that the world of forms is the illusion. A sage on the other hand perceives the formless in the forms. Nirvana is found in the opposites, as it is part of the inseparable universe.

The mystery of duplicity is in everything. The cosmic breath of Brahma cannot be divided. How could we hold on to the in-breath more than the out-breath? We could not, as this is a universal flow of consciousness that expands and contracts in its rhythm and vibrations. The involution and evolution of the individual cannot be fought, as these poles are inseparable. Recognizing that the fabric of reality is made up of all of the apparent opposites brings about a transformation of our mundane view of universal principles such as the Hindu and Buddhist *karma* (which we erroneously associate with a linear version of "cause and effect"), or the Taoist *tzu-jan* (the organic spontaneous universe that just happens with no effort), or *hsiang sheng* (the Taoist term for the mutually arising universe). The label-less master Alan Watts describes karma, tzu-jan, and hsiang sheng in relation to the mystery of duplicity in his eternal treatise *Tao: The Watercourse Way*. He states:

> This is like the Hindu-Buddhist principle of karma—that everything which happens to you is your own action or doing. Thus in many states of mystical experience or cosmic consciousness the difference between what you do and what happens to you, the voluntary and the involuntary, seems to disappear. This feeling may be interpreted as the sense that everything is voluntary—that the whole universe is your own action and will. But this can easily flip into the sense that everything is involuntary. The individual and the will are nothing, and everything that might be called "I" is as much beyond our control as the spinning of the earth in its orbit. But from the Taoist standpoint these two views fall short. They are polar ways of seeing the same truth: that there is no ruler and nothing ruled. What goes on simply happens of itself (*tzu-jan*) without either push or pull, since every push is also a pull and

every pull a push, as in using a steering wheel. This is, then, a transactional view of the world, for as there is no buying without selling, and vice versa, there is no environment without organisms, and vice versa. This is, again, the principle of "mutual arising" (*hsiang sheng*). As the universe produces our consciousness, our consciousness evokes the universe; and this realization transcends and closes the debate between materialists and idealists (or mentalists), determinists and free-willers, who represent the *yin* and the *yang* of philosophical opinion.[2]

Consciousness and the universe cannot exist independent of each other. The mystery of duplicity is interwoven in the fabric of consciousness. We cannot have a sage without a warrior; they are the evolved and involved awareness of the cosmos. There is no good or bad, hot or cold, light or dark, and so on in the real world, as they are all measurements of maya. As soon as we imply that an opposite exists, then duality is maintained. In the belief that things are separate, we are still trying to control the universe. Involution and evolution are inseparable states of consciousness where the knower and the known become one. In pursuit of nirvana we ignorantly attempt to dissect the movements of involution and evolution into separate parts, believing that we must hold on to the true self while ignoring the focusing aspect of the psyche known as the ego. But the mystery of life is that nirvana cannot exist without *samsara*.

Samsara is the Sanskrit word that refers to the "wheel of life" we find ourselves bound to life after life. Samsara is the involution of consciousness or being caught in the detail, which causes suffering. The illusion of maya is within the world of samsara, but samsara is an inseparable part of the universe. Those who wish to transcend samsara in search of nirvana will find themselves perpetually going in circles, as nirvana is not something separate from samsara. They are apparent opposites, like practice and spontaneity or involution and evolution. Samsara is a way of clinging to life and forcing oneself upon life. Nirvana on the other hand is like spontaneity, as it is the state of consciousness in the enlightened mode of the Eternal Now. Yet they are inseparable; they flow in unison with the involution and evolution of consciousness.

Nirvana and samsara are the movements of awareness that the universe expresses. The irony of any spiritual practice is that one is attempting to transcend samsara through implying that it exists and on the other hand trying to attain nirvana by implying it doesn't exist. A jivanmukta has no sense of needing to jump off the wheel of samsara or do anything to attain nirvana. The jivanmukta makes no effort to either transcend samsara or attain nirvana, as both are only assumptions—that samsara is real and that nirvana is somewhere other than within. To a jivanmukta nirvana is samsara; through the evolution of perception, the formless nirvana world is perceived in the world of forms, samsara. This is seeing the infinite in the finite. Nirvana cannot exist without samsara, and vice versa. So the jivanmukta does not take either side. One who is balanced in the center moves in relation to nirvana and samsara without being attached to either, fully receptive to life with no impulse to control any aspect of the universe.

The jivanmukta has let go of everything and lives in the Eternal Now. Even the echoes of the mind, which we call memory, are no longer there. A jivanmukta does not cling to memories of the past or plans for the future. This is the meaning of the unification of nirvana and samsara. Nirvana and samsara are identical essence, which a liberated soul has confirmed in their own being. The eternal treatise of Buddhism known as the *Lankavatara Sutra* points to the non-duality of all things:

> Again, Mahamati, what is meant by non-duality? It means that light and shade, long and short, black and white, are relative terms, Mahamati, and not independent of each other; as Nirvana and Samsara are, all things are not-two. There is no Nirvana except where is Samsara; there is no Samsara except where is Nirvana; for the condition of existence is not of a mutually exclusive character. Therefore it is said that all things are non-dual as are Nirvana and Samsara.[3]

Non-duality is the awareness that all beings will embody if they are sincere in exploring the great work of eternity. Jivanmuktas do not express their liberated state through imposing their will upon anything; instead their consciousness is completely receptive to all experience. This is the essence of humility. Letting go of life has allowed them to receive life. Humility as real strength is realized by a jivanmukta, one who has become a receptive vessel that the source of the universe can flow through. Humility is the human quality that reflects the universe's existence. This is why those who are truthfully humble emanate indescribable power.

11
The Science of Humility

᯽

*T*he fundamental reason we exist as human beings is to find out who we are under the layers of illusion. We are not here to save the world nor start a revolution. These are but projections of the mind into the delusion of maya. The art that is our life is to realize the formless truth of reality in the world of forms. That perception is the only thing that evolves an individual and the only thing that evolves the world. The awe-inspiring wonder of consciousness is that anything you wish to change about the world is something you actually have to change about yourself. The duality of within and without does not exist, so any attempt to change what is perceived without is only a vain ambition of the ego.

As we have seen the physical, mental, and spiritual planes of consciousness are interconnected. In essence they are the same consciousness, which we have intellectually dissected in order to gain complete comprehension. When truthfully assimilated the intellectual interpretation disappears, as the concept of duality has evaporated. The unfoldment of an individual entails a sincere exploration of the great work of eternity, the process an individual goes through to realize separation is an illusion. This leads to the correct awareness of the evolution of perception, to manifesting the universal fragrance known as the science of humility. The science of humility is open to all, but it is not something that can be forced through any practice or method; it is a way of life. One who lives the science of humility is one who resonates with the unceasing harmonic pattern of the cosmos and brings its eternal mystery into the manifest world.

THE INDESCRIBABLE REALITY OF TRUTH

One who lives the science of humility comes into contact with that irreducible essence of the universe that in most wisdom traditions is referred to as "truth." Truth is an inadequate word to describe that which some know and others do not. In the wisdom traditions it refers to the underlying reality of life, which one either experiences or not. Truth is absolute. It is not something that can be pulled to pieces and examined. Something that is spontaneous cannot be analyzed or theorized about, as it is "now" and not anywhere else. The science of humility is the realization that there never were any parts or separate moments in reality.

However, our entire world, which is deluded by the ego and the illusion of maya, teaches the individual to study the parts of the universe as if they were separate. This is a prime reason why many institutions such as science, religion, philosophy, and academia have all got it wrong. In the relative world truth is the opposite of lies; it has no other meaning than this, as all things are transient and not absolute. Most beings associate truth with information interpreted by the ego, under the influence of its conditioning. So truth varies from one to another. This is reflected by the ancient saying, "One man's truth is another man's half-truth."

Information appears good or bad to us based on our conditioning, which is learned. If conditioning is an illusion of the phenomenal world, then what that conditioning is attracted to is far more of an illusion. If we want to be sincere in revealing truth, then we must never live from conditioning. If we become that noble, then all information will have lost its appeal. No information in the world, no matter how poetic, is fundamental truth. In the end conventional knowledge is nothing but ephemeral information. But our conditioning breeds strong opinions in us. And we regard the opinions of others as righteous or ignorant based on whether they resonate with our own view of life. Truth is not something to resonate with nor is it something to have an opinion about; it is beyond the normal realm of anything we can conceive.

Those who have opinions have lost touch with what truth really is. Having an opinion means having an impulse to control life, which is uncontrollable. Those who, not realizing that the universe is spontaneous, go out on a search for truth will never find it if their search is dictated by their opinions. The idea that the world needs to be saved is a conditioned opinion, based on our fears and anxieties, which feed our ego. The opinion of one is the opposite of another, which fuels conflict.

The conflict we experience is actually internal. We need to go through this internal conflict as we slowly learn that we are losing control of our grip on life. Total loss of control is what most of us fear, yet this is a prerequisite in the science of humility. In the great work of eternity, the natural progression is to transcend conditioning, which leaves no opinion to be expressed. A jivan-mukta or sage is one who has completely let go, thus becoming an agendaless being. Only an opinionless being with no agenda can be trusted in this universe.

Truth is not an opinion, a belief, or anything we can categorically put into words. It is not something conceptual nor is it something to be intellectualized. It is felt in the consciousness of an individual. One of the biggest mistakes of many teachers of eternity is to believe truth can be pointed to. In a sense it can be, but the pointing is only to the idea or concept we have of what that single truth is. The idea or concept of truth is not the actual reality of truth. Truth is the Void that transcends time and space. Sometimes a mysterious or nonsensical answer to a concrete question touches on that indescribable truth.

One such case is a famous story of an encounter between a monk and his master, known as Tung-shan Shou-ch'u in Chinese and Tozan Shusho in Japanese. The monk inquired into the nature of his existence and asked Tung-shan, "What is the Buddha?" Tung-shan replied, "Three pounds of flax." Now this will be taken differently according to the hearer's attunement. Some say Tung-shan Shou-ch'u was weighing flax at the time of the question and was demonstrating the spontaneity of life. This may have some remnants of truth in it, but it is not the depth of the question and answer. Tung-shan's irrational answer of "three pounds of flax" is to snap the monk out of a conceptualization of what he is seeking. The answer itself is spontaneous, requiring no prior thought.

The question "What is the Buddha" is seeking an intellectual answer regarding the underlying truth of the universe. To formulate an answer in the form of ideas, concepts, opinions, or any type of thinking would be an insane task. Receiving the answer "three pounds of flax," the monk is left speechless. The expression of no speech comes at that profound moment when the empty silent Void beyond the realm of understanding is experienced. An answer of what or who we truly are is unattainable, if we are seeking a logical conclusion expressed in words. The search for what truth is will always keep us from it, as we are trying to control our experience.

Most of us who are forcing an understanding of truth are doing so with foggy glasses on; we are still perceiving reality according to our conditioning. When death comes our conditioning, opinions, control, concepts, and information will all have to be let go of, because what is coming is unavoidable.

None of these transient aspects of our being will stand the test of time. Before death comes we can let go completely and honestly, to reveal our irreducible essence.

The science of humility is not embodied by our personality; that persona is merely the role we have assumed in this life through our conditioning. The personality or ego is only the accumulation of all concepts, ideas, opinions, and information we identify with. All of this borrowed identity has to be let go of to reveal the true self. We cling to this idea of who we are, and so we suffer because of it. The wisdom traditions reveal that our grasping hold on our identity is what binds us to the wheel of birth and death known as samsara, where we live life after life, dealing forever and ever with our past life karma. Instead of sinking into the ocean of consciousness, we continuously find ourselves riding the waves of identity where we are hypnotized by our projections, judgments, and desires. No one in this world escapes the ignorance of conditioning, but there are those very few who become free of its clutches.

ONE WILL

Liberation or freedom can be perceived in a being whose humility is parallel with the receptive principle of the universe. For eons this feminine principle has been suppressed and thought of as inferior to the masculine-dominated psyche of the masses. This indoctrinated illusion causes neurosis within the psyche of individuals who associate their beliefs with love. The illusion of maya leads us to believe that we love separate parts of reality, which means that we do not really love, but are still measuring the immeasurable. Loving an individual or some object is conditioned by ideas and opinions about how the other and object should be. This is not attuned with the receptive nature of the universe, so it cannot be humility or love. What love truly is cannot be experienced unless one is humbly receptive to all experience. Those who know truthfully that love is unconditional, will let go of love, that is, the common conceptual idea of love. In the great work of eternity, if they can truly let love go, then their real love will become present. This is the science of humility. A jivanmukta loves and nourishes all beings.

Having let go of the concept of separation, the jivanmukta does not interfere with the course of all things and entities in the universe. The jivanmukta is at the center of the circle, which is a mirror of the center of the universe that simply watches the transient world rise and fall. One who is in the true position of the center perceives the great happening of life in its vibration and rhythm. Humility allows the universe to be what it is, looking upon it with the same clarity as the child who sees the world with no boundaries. As the dance of chaos continues, the humble individual is unfazed, as they do not doubt their own experience.

The science of humility is trusting one's own innate nature in correspondence to the whole, where all experience is perceived as the functioning of universal harmony. This can only be proven within one's own being. Those ignorant of the science of humility will seek to judge one who has shed the power of the ego, as this threatens the illusions they cling to. But the divinities or sages of antiquity who have lived the science of humility have etched a lasting memory in the collective consciousness. This is the evidence of the eternal truth that emanates from a being who is receptive to all experiences without holding on to any. The divinities, sages, and jivanmuktas all went through their own trials and tribulations until they reached the point of complete despair. Then they realized in a moment that all their vain attempts to change or save the world were based on their agenda for others. In this enlightening moment they realized that from the beginning there had been nothing to do, as what they were searching for had never left them. In their spontaneous enlightenment the clarity of the evolution of perception could be seen in all things. The total release of their will lets the Void express its mysterious dharma.

A jivanmukta who assimilated the science of humility so completely was the holy sage Sri Ramana Maharshi, who renounced all worldly attachments at the young age of sixteen. Sri Ramana Maharshi left his family with no notice after a profound experience of feeling that he was going to die turned him totally inward to the great work of eternity. After this experience he set out on a journey to reside at the foot of the sacred mountain in India known most affectionately as "Arunachala." Once he arrived at Arunachala, he took a vow of silence for many years. After a long search his mother finally found him and pleaded with him to speak, to explain why he left. But, unmoving in his serenity, he simply wrote a brief message on a piece of paper. This message exemplifies humility and the receptive nature of the universe:

> The ordainer controls the fate of souls in accordance with their *prarabdha karma*. Whatever is destined not to happen will not happen, try as you may. Whatever is destined to happen will happen, do what you may to prevent it. This is certain. The best course, therefore, is to remain silent.[1]

After this reunion his mother left with no intellectual answers; she was frustrated at their auspicious meeting. But to the astonishment of most, Sri Ramana Maharshi's mother returned years later, not in an effort to claim back her child, but to become his disciple. Such is the power of the science of humility.

In the spontaneity of the Eternal Now, the science of humility reveals that even though most individuals believe they have a will of their own, they actually don't; these are all the accumulations of past conditioning. The individual will is actually a mirage, another illusion of maya, because a separate ego does not exist. The unification of the individual and Divine Will is the realization that there was only ever the Divine Will working through us. The only difference is we are either conscious of this or we still believe we are in control of our life.

Realizing that the whole idea of who we think we are can never be in our control is a profound awakening, isolated to our focal point of consciousness. As we have explained truth is not an idea, concept, belief, or anything else. The individual will is built on these phantoms, so how could this be who we are? Who we truly are is beyond anything we can conceive. The true self is not something we can point to or put into words. It is experienced by the individual who can confirm there is only the true self and no other separate will or ego. The waves of identity are the illusion of the ocean in separate motion; the correct perception is that what is moving the wave into motion is the ocean itself. The wave is not independent of the ocean and likewise our will is not independent from the truth that underlies all of reality. What we have then is one will moving through all life. An individual is a focal point of that single consciousness that expresses itself in its infinite substance that we mistakenly call duality.

Regardless of whether we want to let go or not, there is no "I" who is in control, making choices for our life. We have apparent choice, but we really have no choice, as the universe happens of itself and we are not outside of that. The science of humility is the foundational cornerstone for realizing the receptive nature of the universe. Nothing humbles a being more than realizing that what will be will be, or in other words, what happens in our life is beyond our control. We can either learn to flow with it or can continue to fight it. Either way it is already mapped out for us.

In the ancient symbolism of Gautama the Buddha, we find the grandest demonstration of the science of humility. He holds his hand open or with a bowl receiving alms, showing a complete trust in the universe with receptivity to all experience. This symbolism has nothing to do with asking for anything from anybody, which is the assumption of one who only sees the world superficially. The Buddha and alms symbolism is esoterically known as the receptive principle of the universe, the feminine (see figure 11.1).

Figure 11.1. Gautama the Buddha

Gautama the Buddha, being a male in a receptive feminine posture, symbolizes the occult wisdom that unifies the masculine and feminine principles of the universe in an individual who emanates the virtue of the science of humility. This indicates a trust in which one is not chasing life or attempting to impose one's will; humility is embodied not as a concept but as a universal reality.

The science of humility is not something you can choose to bring into your consciousness. On the contrary, you need to let go of everything you believe is real in order to know the science of humility. All that stands in the way of your liberation from the shackles of separation that imprison you is a ghost; you just need to let go. But paradoxically you cannot intentionally attempt to let go or unintentionally attempt to let go; it must be as natural as growing hair. The real you is not a puppet that life pushes around, because the deep down real you is the entire universe. Everything is changing, everything is moving. Your thoughts are changing, your emotions are changing, and your body is changing, but who is the witness of change? Is it not you? Find out and reveal the truth of who you are. There is nothing to gain or renounce, nothing to learn or unlearn. In truth there is no one to liberate or free; knowing this is the science of humility.

Notes

INTRODUCTION

1. Watts, *The Way of Zen,* 101.

I. THE GREAT WORK OF ETERNITY

1. Lao-tzu, *Tao Te Ching,* chapter 78.
2. Three Initiates, *The Kybalion,* 28.
3. Prabhupada, *Bhagavad Gita As It Is,* 337–38.

2. THE PHYSICAL CANVAS

1. Mouravieff, *Gnosis,* 68.
2. Three Initiates, *The Kybalion,* 39.
3. Lao-tzu, *Tao Te Ching,* chapter 1.
4. Aun Weor, *Introduction to Gnosis,* cover.

3. THE MENTAL CALLIGRAPHY

1. Yukteswar, *The Holy Science,* 7–8.
2. Three Initiates, *The Kybalion,* 43.

3. Atkinson, *Mind Power,* 352.

4. Three Initiates, *The Kybalion,* 30.

5. Yukteswar, *The Holy Science,* 23.

6. Three Initiates, *The Kybalion,* 147.

7. Dictionary.com, "Cognitive Dissonance," http://dictionary.reference .com/browse/cognitive+dissonance?s=t

4. THE EVOLUTION OF PERCEPTION

1. Wilhelm, *The I Ching,* 78.

2. Maharaj, *I Am That,* 148.

5. THE WAY OF THE WARRIOR AND PATH OF THE SAGE

1. Prabhupada, *Bhagavad Gita As It Is,* 561–63.

2. Watts, *The Way of Zen,* 26.

6. PRIMAL RHYTHM

1. Dyer, *Wisdom of the Ages,* 35.

2. de Salzmann, *The Reality of Being,* 297.

3. Wilhelm, *The I Ching,* introduction, lv.

4. Three Initiates, *The Kybalion,* 53.

5. Ibid., 35.

7. PATTERNED VIBRATION

1. Aun Weor, *The Divine Science,* 11.

2. Russell, *A New Concept of the Universe,* 111, 127, and 128.

3. Watts, *The Way of Zen,* 32.

8. THE HYPNOSIS OF DUALITY

1. Tsu, *Chuang Tsu,* 29.
2. Lao-tzu, *Tao Te Ching,* chapter 2.
3. Dattatreya, *Song of the Avadhut,* 87.
4. Watts, *The Way of Zen,* 38.

9. NOW IS THE HOUSE OF SPONTANEITY

1. Suzuki, *Zen Mind, Beginner's Mind,* 13.
2. Watts, *Do You Do It, or Does It Do You.*

10. AT THE CENTER OF THE UNIVERSE IS A JIVANMUKTA

1. Watts, *The Way of Zen,* 125.
2. Watts, *Tao,* 53.
3. Suzuki, *The Lankavatara Sutra,* 67–68.

11. THE SCIENCE OF HUMILITY

1. Maharshi, *Saddarsanam and An Inquiry into the Revelation,* 218.

Bibliography

Atkinson, William Walker. *Mind Power: The Secret of Mental Magic.* New York: Cosimo, 2007.

Aun Weor, Samael. *The Divine Science: Eternal Techniques of Authentic Mysticism.* New York: Glorian, 2009.

———. *Introduction to Gnosis: Gnostic Methods for Today's World.* New York: Glorian, 2009.

———. *The Spiritual Power of Sound: The Awakening of Consciousness and the Laws of Nature.* New York: Glorian, 2011.

———. *Tarot & Kabbalah: The Path of Initiation in the Sacred Arcana.* New York: Glorian, 2010.

Braden, Gregg. *The Divine Matrix: Bridging Time, Space, Miracles, and Belief.* Carlsbad, Calif.: Hay House, 2008.

Dattatreya. *Dattatreya's Song of the Avadhut.* Translated by Swami Abhayananda. Delhi, India: Sri Satguru, 2000.

de Salzmann, Jeanne. *The Reality of Being: The Fourth Way of Gurdjieff.* Boston, Mass.: Shambhala, 2011.

Dyer, Wayne W. *Wisdom of the Ages: 60 Days to Enlightenment.* New York: William Morrow, 2002.

Easwaran, Eknath, trans. *The Upanishads.* Tomales, Calif.: Nilgiri Press, 2007.

Fersen, Eugene. *Science of Being.* Sumas, Wash.: The Lightbearers Publishing, LLC, 2011.

Lao-tzu. *Tao Te Ching: An Illustrated Journey*. Translated by Stephen Mitchell. London: Frances Lincoln, 2009.

Lipton, Bruce H. *The Biology of Belief: Unleashing the Power of Consciousness, Matter & Miracles*. Carlsbad, Calif.: Hay House, 2008.

Maharaj, Sri Nisargadatta. *I Am That*. Mumbai, India: Chetana, 1973.

Maharshi, Sri Ramana. *Saddarsanam and An Inquiry into the Revelation of Truth and Oneself*. Translated by Nome. Santa Cruz, Calif.: Society of Abidance in Truth, 2009.

Mouravieff, Boris. *Gnosis: Study and Commentaries on the Esoteric Tradition of Eastern Orthodoxy, Book 1, Exoteric Cycle*. Chicago, Ill.: Praxis Institute Press, 1989.

Ouspensky, P. D. *In Search of the Miraculous: The Teachings of G. I. Gurdjieff*. Orlando, Fla.: Harcourt, 2001.

Prabhupada, A. C. Bhaktivedanta Swami. *Bhagavad Gita As It Is*. Los Angeles: The Bhaktivedanta Book Trust, 1983.

Ramacharaka, Yogi. *Advance Course in Yogi Philosophy and Oriental Occultism*. Chicago, Ill.: The Yogi Publication Society, 1931.

Ramamoorthy, H., and Nome. *The Song of Ribhu: Translated from the Original Tamil Version of the Ribhu Gita*. Santa Cruz, Calif.: Society of Abidance in Truth, 2000.

Russell, Walter. *A New Concept of the Universe*. Waynesboro, Va.: The University of Science and Philosophy, 1989.

Steiner, Rudolf. *Outline of Occult Science*. New York: Cambridge University Press, 2011.

Suzuki, Daisetz Teitaro, trans. *The Lankavatara Sutra: A Mahayana Text*. Philadelphia, Pa.: Coronet Books, 1999.

Suzuki, Shunryu. *Zen Mind, Beginner's Mind*. Boston, Mass.: Shambhala, 2011.

Three Initiates. *The Kybalion: Hermetic Philosophy*. Chicago, Ill.: The Yogi Publication Society, 1940.

Tsu, Chuang. *Chuang Tsu: Inner Chapters, A Companion Volume to Tao Te Ching*. Translated by Gia-Fu Feng and Jane English. Portland, Oreg.: Amber Lotus, 2008.

Watts, Alan. *Do You Do It, or Does It Do You: How to Let the Universe Meditate You.* Audio CD. Louisville, Colo.: Sounds True, 2005.

———. *Tao: The Watercourse Way.* New York: Pantheon, 1977.

———. *The Way of Zen.* New York: Vintage Books, 1999.

Wilhelm, Richard. *The I Ching, or Book of Changes.* Princeton, N.J.: Princeton University Press, 1967.

———. *The Secret of the Golden Flower: A Chinese Book of Life.* London: Arkana, 1984.

Yukteswar, Swami Sri. *The Holy Science.* Los Angeles: Self-Realization Fellowship, 1990.

Index

Page numbers in *italics* indicate illustrations.

material versus spiritual aspects,
55–56
of perception, xv, 56–58, 61–62,
95
real nature of, 16–20
eye of Brahma, 29

fear, xiv, 11–14, 109
feminine principle, 15–16, 81–82,
112–13, 137, 142
formless reality, 5, 6–7, 96, 132
freemasonry, Seal of Scottish Rite,
58–59, *58*

galactic harmonics, 30–32
gender, 28–30. *See also* feminine
principle; masculine principle
General Law, 25–26
Gnosis, 25–26
Gospel of Thomas, 59
grand center, 29–30
Gurdjieff, George Ivanovich,
78–79

harmony
of human body, 35–36
living in, 23–24
perceiving, 58, 62, 76
seeing in all things, 54
universal, 35
Hermes Trismegistus
Caduceus of, 60–61, *60*
Principle of Correspondence (As
above, so below), 17–20, 31

Principle of Gender, 28–30
Principle of Rhythm, 83–85
Principle of Vibration, 45
Hinduism, 59–60
Holy Science, The, 41, 45–46
human body, 34, 35–36
human harmonics, 33–34
humility, 8–9, 14, 15–16

I Ching (Book of Changes), 54,
80–82, 115
intelligent harmonics, 35–36
involution, 78, 79–80, 106, 128,
129, 130
irreducible essence, 5–6, 21–22

Jesus Christ, 59, 61
jivanmukta, 120–21, 135, 137, 138

karma, 42, 128–29
Krishna, 65
kundalini energy, 60–61
Kybalion, The, 42, 83

Lankavatara Sutra, 131
Lao-tzu, 71–72, *72*. *See also Tao Te
Ching*
law
of attraction, 121
of change, 76–80, 82–83, 93
general, 25–26
of octaves, 78–79
of three, 82
See also Hermes Trismegistus